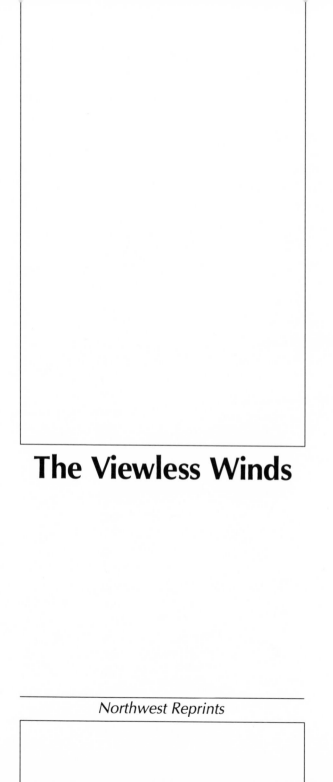

The Viewless Winds

Northwest Reprints

Northwest Reprints
Series Editor: Robert J. Frank

Other titles in the series:

The Viewless Winds

Murray Morgan

Introduction by Harold Simonson

Oregon State University Press
Corvallis, Oregon

The paper in this book meets the guidelines for permanence and durability of the Committee on Production Guidelines for Book Longevity of the Council on Library Resources and the minimum requirements of the American National Standard for Permanence of Paper for Printed Library Materials Z39.48-1984.

Library of Congress Cataloging-in-Publication Data
Morgan, Murray Cromwell, 1916-
The viewless winds / Murray Morgan: introduction by Harold Simonson.
p. cm. — (Northwest reprints)
Reprint. Originally published: New York: Dutton, 1949.
ISBN 0-87071-504-6. (alk. paper)
ISBN 0-87071-505-4 (pbk.) (alk. paper)
I. Title. II. Series.
PS3563.O8714V54 1990
813'.54—dc20   89-16355
                                                          CIP

PREFACE

                                but there were things
That covered what a man was, and set him apart
From others, things by which others knew him. The place
Where he lived, the horse he rode, his relatives, his wife,
His voice, complexion, beard, politics, religion or lack of it,
And so on. With time, these things fall away
Or dwindle into shadows: river sand blowing away
From some long-buried old structure of bleached boards
That appears a vague shadow through the sand-haze,
        and then stands clear,
Naked, angular, itself.
            from "Trial and Error," H.L. Davis

People new to a region are especially interested in what things might set them apart from others. In works by Northwest writers, we get to know about the place where we live, about each other, about our history and culture, and about our flora and fauna. And with time, some things about ourselves start to come into focus out of the shadows of our history.

To give readers an opportunity to look into the place where Northwesterners live, the Oregon State University Press is making available again many books that are out of print. The Northwest Reprints Series will reissue a range of books, both fiction and nonfiction. Books will be selected for different reasons: some for their literary merit, some for their historical significance, some for provocative concerns, and some for these and other reasons together. Foremost, however, will be the book's potential to interest a range of readers who are curious about the region's voice and complexion. The Northwest Reprints Series will make works of well-known and lesser-known writers available for all.

                                        RJF

                                                v

Introduction

Studs Terkel says that his book *Working* (1974), "being about work, is, by its very nature, about violence—to the spirit as well as the body" (ix). Compiling what a broad spectrum of ordinary workers had to say about their daily jobs, Terkel found the common element to be ulcers, accidents, shouting-matches, fistfights, and nervous breakdowns as well as "kicking the dog around"—Terkel's metaphor for the humiliations, both psychic and physical, that bedevil the search for daily meaning and bread. One worker grumbles, "The system stinks"; another, "You can't sock General Motors . . . you can't sock a system"; another, "Most of us, like the assembly line worker, have jobs that are too small for our spirit" (xxii-xxiv).

Something of this same violence pervades Murray Morgan's *The Viewless Winds* (1949), its title taking on universality from Shakespeare's lines in *Measure for Measure:*

> *To be imprison'd in the viewless winds,*
> *And blown with restless violence round about*
> *The pendent world (III, i, 124-126).*

It's not a pleasant image. In it one senses the willy-nilly nature of things. Persons who deny it are often fanatics and pathological optimists, their vision made deceptively clear by greed or the certainty of moral rightness. Shifting ambiguity, on the other hand, recommends wariness, cynicism, and detachment. Whether the system is social, economic, political, or moral—and whether survival in it depends upon competition, compromise, or moral struggle—Terkel and Morgan are not alone in saying that some kind of violence seems to oil human affairs.

Violence done to soul and body is a common theme in American literature, starting back with America's first significant novelist, Charles Brockden Brown, whose turn-of-the-(eighteenth)-century novels exude murder and madness. In *Walden* (1849), Henry David Thoreau addresses men and women everywhere who, in paying the soul-stuff the system demands, end up violating their true selves. Herman Melville says such persons take up "pistol and ball" (against themselves or others) or go to sea where, ironically, violence only increases. As for Walt Whitman, Confederate guns of April firing on Fort Sumter shattered his melodious work anthems, and his *Democratic Vistas* (1871) left little doubt that violence did not end when Generals Grant and Lee shook hands. Capitalism spawned it too. Mark Twain puzzled at how James Fenimore Cooper's Natty Bumppo, the archetypal frontiersman who harmonized with the ways of nature, could ever superintend one of Andrew Carnegie's steel mills. Twain saw that American capitalism, nurtured by frontier ideals, had turned into something all too natural, like a jungle. In *A Connecticut Yankee in King Arthur's Court* (1889), Twain visualized the fictional Hank Morgan as Natty Bumppo's reincarnation, now the superintendent of Hartford's Colt arms factory manufacturing Gatling guns capable of firing 600 shots a minute, with one pull of the trigger, and of creating an Armageddon of faultless killing.

Finding Twain's fancy amusing, his admirers paid to attend public lectures of this curmudgeon dressed in white linen. Often left unheard was his savage mockery of a system that permitted, in 1890, 9 percent of the American people to own 71 percent of the nation's money. Twain thought this situation violent too. By 1900, 1 percent owned 50 percent of the wealth and the top 12 percent controlled 90 percent. Average pay for unskilled workers was $10 a week, for ten to twelve hours of labor each day, six days a week. Factories were badly lighted and ventilated, with no attempt made to guard workers against dangerous machinery. Compensation for death or injury was virtually unknown. All the while, robber barons and their political cohorts preached a gospel of wealth that defended Darwinian inequality.

In the forefront of protest movements demanding reform and government restrictions were labor unions, first in the 1860s the National Labor Union and, twenty years later, the Knights of Labor and the American Federation of Labor with a combined membership of a million workers. By 1900 AFL members alone numbered more than two million. Political radicals organized the Socialist Labor Party in 1877. Eugene V. Debs formed the Socialist Party, which polled 95,000 votes in the national election of 1900, and nearly a million in the election of 1912. During these tumultuous years Farmers' Alliances joined the Populist Party, led by intellectuals Henry George, Lester F. Ward, Thorstein Veblen, and Herbert Croly. Elizabeth Cady Stanton and Susan B. Anthony spearheaded the women's struggle for political equality.

Protesters marched in the streets, others engaged in strikes, boycotts, sabotage, and riots. The most notorious riot occurred in Chicago's Haymarket Square on May 4, 1886, during a mass protest against the earlier killing of International Harvester strikers by police. Someone threw a bomb into a column of police, killing seven and wounding sixty more. Out in the Northwest, the mining and lumbering towns roared with gunfire and dynamite. William D. "Big Bill" Haywood, who spearheaded the International Workers of the World, was put on trial in 1906 for complicity in the dynamite-bomb murder of Idaho's ex-Governor

Frank Steuenberg. Desperate because of layoffs, hunger, insufficient wages, and loss of self-respect, IWW members (Wobblies) shut down sawmills and logging camps. The most publicized skirmishes involving Wobblies were the "massacres" at Everett in 1916 and Centralia in 1919. Stopped at the Everett dock by Sheriff Donald McCrea, a boatload of some 150 Wobblies from Seattle answered with gunshots aimed at the sheriff's well-armed deputies who returned the gunfire, leaving half a dozen Wobblies dead and nearly thirty wounded. In Centralia, uniformed American Legionnaires attacked Wobblies watching a patriotic parade; several were beaten, one was hanged from a railroad bridge, and the others were sent to prison.

We use the label "realism" to describe the literature paralleling this widespread civil strife. Like other labels it may simplify reality and take on a tyrannical plausibility. However, the underlying principle of American literary realism was to write about everyday people, not romantic heroes and heroines but ordinary citizens, usually the workers, the obscure flotsam in the social mass, the poor, the underdog, the "imprison'd" buffeted by the "viewless winds" of fate or, more realistically, by some fat-cat factory owner, banker, or congressman whose concerns favored the wealthy 1 percent.

The writer who best illustrates this social awakening is not Twain but his friend, William Dean Howells, editor of the *Atlantic Monthly* and prolific novelist. To him, the 1886 Haymarket Riot brought to a boil the simmering influence of Tolstoy and the American social reformer Henry George, both widely read by young realist writers. Turning to socialism and realistic fiction, Howells wrote in rapid succession *Annie Kilburn* (1889), *A Hazard of New Fortune* (1890), and

The Quality of Mercy (1892), in which he indicts a morally decayed system that pits wealth against labor. He later championed naturalists Stephen Crane and Frank Norris whose novels explored deeper undersides of both social and psychological realism. Similarly, in *Main-Travelled Roads* (1891), Hamlin Garland described farmers' agony caused by banks and speculators. Muckrakers Ida Tarbell, Jacob A. Riis, Upton Sinclair, and Lincoln Steffens exposed corruption among oil, railroad, and meatpacking magnates, and among politicians from the smallest Chicago wards to the halls of Congress.

The Depression of the 1930s seemed to signal the collapse of the whole system. Two books—one published early in the decade and the other just prior to the economic turnabout fostered by World War II—capture the violence of American class struggle. In his *Autobiography* (1931), Steffens tells how his journalistic career convinced him that corruption is at the heart of government and business. Capitalism is the villain. "I have seen the future," he said after a visit to Bolshevik Russia, "and it works." The other book is John Steinbeck's *The Grapes of Wrath* (1939), depicting the violence to both body and soul that an inhuman system brings to its victims. About his own early days of journalism, my long-time Tacoma-born friend Murray Morgan says, "If I had heroes back in those days, they were Steffens and Steinbeck and all the working stiffs."

ἐᾱ ἐᾱ ἐᾱ

From 1937 to 1939 Morgan was a reporter and then managing editor for Hoquiam's *Grays Harbor Washingtonian*. After brief periods as secretary of Seattle Municipal League and reporter for the *Spokane Chronicle,* he returned in 1940 to the Hoquiam newspaper and almost at once was caught up in reporting the

Laura Law murder case. Wife of an Aberdeen labor leader (Hoquiam and Aberdeen are contiguous towns in Grays Harbor County), Law was bludgeoned to death in her home on the night of January 5, 1940. Some townspeople insisted her husband, Dick Law, was the prime suspect even though union members testified he had been attending a local union meeting at the time of her death. That everyone knew of his efforts to make the labor movement more radical did little to enhance his credibility. He himself charged that her murder was linked to the region's labor and political conflicts. He numbered foes among not only the local business leaders (Aberdeen's so-called Business Builders) but also the anticommunist factions within the AFL's Sawmill and Timberworkers Union and his own International Woodworkers of America. That the case was never solved gave it added mystery for newspaperman and novelist Morgan who recreated it in *The Viewless Winds,* written during the winter of 1946-47 while he and his wife Rosa lived on Puget Sound's Maury Island.*

In the novel, Morgan wanted to separate the murder from the local circumstances surrounding it, and concentrate on how the reaction split the community. With the disclaimer that characters and incidents "do not represent actual persons, events or places," Morgan transforms his imaginary town of Cove into a metaphor of social and political turmoil typical of that found in countless American towns and cities. He makes the murder secondary to the violence that follows when radical reformers and their cadre of working stiffs challenge the system. Set in the 1930s, it is a stark proletarian novel that describes the community life of Grays Harbor torn apart by opposing social

* *For a full account of the actual incident, see Saltvig.*

and economic forces, corruption, and hopelessness. With the nearby hills stripped of Douglas-fir forests and the town's western flank exposed to the ocean's violent rainstorms, Cove is no longer what its name bespeaks. This irony is matched by a further one, namely that the murder of Dee Dawson, wife of Cove's labor leader Bull Dawson, is well-nigh irrelevant to the novel's deeper theme. The violence committed by the murderer, a drunken "beach rat" with nothing at stake in the divided town, exposes violence that already exists. Furthermore, the murderer whom the towns-people seek in Cove stalks among them as part and parcel of themselves.

⪧ ⪧ ⪧

By the 1930s, the West Coast lumber industry had decimated men and timber at an appalling rate. The record shows violence committed against the land by the loggers and reciprocal violence to their own life and limb (cf. Prouty). The magnitude of Grays Harbor lumbering can be seen in the number of mills and logging operations. Starting with five waterpowered sawmills from 1852 to 1880, the Harbor sprouted seven steam plants in the next five years. By the end of the century sawmills were built at the edge of tide-water on both banks of the Chehalis River from Cosmopolis and Aberdeen to Hoquiam, and up the Wishkaw and Hoquiam rivers. According to historian Edwin Van Syckle, "a tallyman could have counted 46 log-using outfits on tidewater: sawmills, shingle mills and specialty mills"(263). For two decades into the new century Grays Harbor listened to the roar of major "lumber-gushing" operations.

Close at hand were labor unions although, with the exception of the IWW, they never exerted much pres-sure in the lumber industry before World War I. In

1903 the AFL chartered the Shingle Weavers' Union and two years later the International Brotherhood of Woodsmen and Sawmill Workers. These and other unions waxed and waned, their most numerous locals situated in the Puget Sound and Grays Harbor region. Generally, conditions induced only sullen endurance and resignation among the workers. But in 1917 they erupted in widespread strikes against intransigent owners who denied employees an eight-hour day, adequate wage scales, and collective bargaining to improve conditions. The common work day was ten hours, sometimes sixteen, and the extra hours brought no extra pay. In logging camps rude shacks served as bunk houses for twenty or more men, with no facilities for bathing or drying clothes. Cook shacks swarmed with flies from nearby open latrines and garbage pits (see Tyler).

These 1917 clashes culminated ten years of IWW agitation throughout the Northwest that saw wildcat strikes, red-flag parades, free-speech fights, jailhouse hunger strikes, and soapbox oratory which often ended with broken skulls. In the years that followed, business and government leaders warned against the threat of Bolshevism. On one occasion, a mob of "patriotic" vigilantes broke into Aberdeen's IWW hall and dragged out cartloads of records for a festive bonfire. Another mob captured six Aberdeen Wobblies, beat them, and made them kiss the American flag. Washington's Governor Ernest Lister proposed a state-wide organization of vigilantes, a "Patriotic League," to round up Wobblies. United States Attorney-General A. Mitchell Palmer inspired Palmer Raids on aliens and various radical groups all over the nation, using the Pacific Northwest Wobblies as "experimental guinea pigs" (Tyler, p. 148).

By the 1930s Aberdeen staggered under hopeless economic depression. Furthermore, nasty conflicts raged between business and labor, and within labor's own ranks between the AFL and the new, powerful CIO (Congress of Industrial Organization, an affiliate of the militant IWA). This latter schism divided the largely Finnish population of workers into Red Finns (socialist-leaning) and White Finns (conservative). Both groups, however, held Aberdeen's "alien" Poles and Slavs (further divided between Croatians and Serbs) as the common enemy.

Here was realism of desperate people struggling to keep body and soul together, yet questioning and often challenging the very foundations of citizenship. Placed within this shredding social fabric, Morgan's novel stands alongside Clara Weatherwax's *Marching! Marching!* (1930) and Robert Cantwell's *Land of Plenty* (1934), both written as proletarian protests against conditions suffered by lumber workers in Washington's Grays Harbor during the 1930s. Morgan's book contributes to the Northwest literary tradition of labor novels that includes Mary H. Foote's *Coeur d'Alene* (1894) and James Stevens's classic *Big Jim Turner* (1948). The larger perspective includes such protest novelists as Rebecca Harding Davis, Frank Harris, Robert Herrick, Jack Conroy, Harriet W. Gilfillan, and Howard Fast. Rising above all these is John Steinbeck. According to Morgan, the novel that loomed largest for him among Steinbeck's work was not *The Grapes of Wrath* but his earlier *In Dubious Battle* (1936).

ঽ ঽ ঽ

Obvious differences exist between *In Dubious Battle* and *The Viewless Winds*. While both are strike novels, one is set amid California's apple orchards, the other in a fog-shrouded Washington lumbering town. Action for Steinbeck is more physically violent, emotions more visible, antagonism between workers and the "system" more ideological, and the whole drama more panoramic. Morgan uses labor unrest as background for a narrower focus where the central action takes place not in the sawmills and streets but in the mill manager's candlelit dining room, the back shop of the newspaper office, the courtroom, police station, barroom, union hall, beach shack, and a blacked-out grocery store in the dead of night. Steinbeck's action is more out in the open, its fanaticism more intense. Morgan's intrigue festers in the town's shadowy places. Fog and rain send his people to the inside world of spying and blackmail, maligning and bribes—a world where mill manager Gordon Gentry has learned "the purchase price of a moral man with a small bank balance [is] lower than that of an immoral man with money."

Ostensibly the main action involves Dee Dawson's murder and the town's search for her killer. But Morgan employs the surface plot to probe into the real motives of town leaders. Gentry seeks to implicate Bull Dawson in order to break the union. Dawson's supporters, on the other hand, blame Cove's business community and Gentry himself. Union secretary Arne Toivenen, a "devout" Communist whose father was killed in a strike riot at Astoria, makes the human tragedy abstract in order to fulfill the "dramatic possibilities" of Dee Dawson's funeral and demonstrate working-class unity. Although the murder touches everyone, the novel's theme is of a splintered town corrupt at all levels. No one is exempt: not the mill owner Herman Peterson, his son-in-law Gordon Gentry, newspaper owner Rutherford B. Olson, Police Chief Roger Show, Coroner Xenophon Jones, patrolman Will Elliott, or newspaper reporter Gale Seward.

Seward is the novel's central intelligence. He is the one who tries to see all sides and yet remain untouched. As a newspaperman and recent graduate of the University of Missouri School of Journalism, he has learned the "game": get the story but stay emotionally out of it. This lesson means that Seward takes no sides even if his bias favors the union. It means he will defend the unsavory Peterson and Gentry while turning away from Elliott's plea to help change things for the better. Seward is emphatically a newspaperman, not a reformer: "Nobody had hired him to change anything." He loved the daily *Logger* but cared little for Cove, which to him was like a mason's quarry that supplies him with stone. Thus Seward was pleased with the bold headline that topped the morning edition: "Labor Leader's Wife Slain." With a snap of his fingers he boasted, "Best story we've had in one hell of a time."

Having no allegiances as a reporter except to facts, Seward resembles Steinbeck's Doc Burton who stands apart to observe the apple pickers' plight but refuses to join them. Emotional detachment gives Burton the luxury to theorize about social ills, analyzing them as a scientist does a disease. But objectivity, supposedly necessary for science, transforms him into a misanthropic nihilist working towards nothing. He reasons that he's too wise to hope for a better world or to suppose life is anything but brief, its destiny pitiless and dark. At best any battle for social justice is a dubious one because neither side has moral superiority. The side that justifies its ends through violence is no better than the other that does the same. Moreover, tomorrow's system that replaces today's cannot withstand the slow, sure doom that falls on all systems alike. As for today, the only certainty is the moral corruption that holds sway everywhere. What's left for the individual person is to fight, compromise, laugh or cry.

Although Seward doesn't brood like Steinbeck's Doc Burton, he nevertheless remembers the haunting words spoken by patrolman Elliott: "Do you have to be hired to change things?" That the lurching old Syl Freitas has now confessed to the murder means nothing to the deeper issue. Teetering between hope and its futility, the journalist who resolved to remain untouched by events in Cove is the one affected the most. The final scene that takes place in Gordon Gentry's elegant house on the hill suggests novelist Morgan's tilt: acrimony, threats, and secret scheming promise to go on and on.

🙐 🙐 🙐

In recalling the 1930s, Murray Morgan thinks that most Progressive newspapermen were "morally agnostic." Like his hero Lincoln Steffens, they were crusaders as well as cynics. In 1948 Morgan himself grew disillusioned with Progressive doctrinaire ideology even as he served as Washington State's campaign manager for presidential candidate Henry Wallace. It's an ambivalence both politics and journalism require.

Born in 1916, Morgan started newspaper work as a student at Tacoma's Stadium High School where he was graduated in 1933. Four years later he was editor of the University of Washington *Daily*. After two stints in Hoquiam and a kayaking trip down the Danube with his bride Rosa, he earned an M.A. in journalism at Columbia University. While a graduate student, he held jobs at *Time* magazine, CBS World News, and the *New York Herald Tribune* working at *Time* during the day, CBS on the graveyard shift, and the *Tribune* on the weekends. Rosa attended his university classes and he took the exams! Winning a Pulitzer Fellowship allowed them a year in Mexico after which he joined

Time and later the U.S. Army which assigned him
World War II duties in remote outposts of Alaska's
Aleutian Islands. He returned to Tacoma where, during
the City of Destiny's heyday of political corruption in
the 1950s, Morgan worked as both print and radio
news reporter. He continued his daily radio broadcasts
for 22 years, signing off in 1979. He also taught journalism at the University of Puget Sound and Pacific
Northwest history at Tacoma Community College.
He continues as free-lance reviewer and author.

His many books include *Bridge to Russia* (1947)
about the "amazing" Aleutians; *Dixie Raider* (1948),
the saga of the *C. S. S. Shenandoah; The Columbia*
(1949), a history of the River country; *Skid Road*
(1951), best-selling informal history of Seattle; *The
Dam* (1954), a story about Grand Coulee; *Last Wilder-
ness* (1956) about Washington's Olympic Peninsula;
One Man's Gold Rush (1967) about the Klondike
stampede; and *Puget's Sound* (1979), a historical
narrative of early Tacoma and southern Puget Sound.

Harold Simonson

Bibliography

Prouty, Andrew Mason. *More Deadly Than War: Pacific Coast Logging.* New York: Garland, 1985.

Saltvig, Robert. "The Tragic Legend of Laura Law." *Pacific Northwest Quarterly* 78 (July 1987): 91-99.

Terkel, Studs. *Working.* New York: Pantheon, 1974.

Tyler, Robert L. *Rebels in the Woods: The IWW in the Pacific Northwest.* Eugene: University of Oregon, 1967.

Van Syckle, Edwin. *They Tried To Cut It All.* Aberdeen, Washington: Friends of the Aberdeen Public Library, 1980.

THE
VIEWLESS
WINDS

BY

MURRAY MORGAN

E. P. DUTTON & CO., INC.

PUBLISHERS · 1949 · NEW YORK

Copyright, 1949, By Murray Morgan
All rights reserved

❧

PRINTED IN THE UNITED STATES OF AMERICA
BY THE WILLIAM BYRD PRESS, INC.
RICHMOND, VIRGINIA

For Gene and for Rosa

To be imprison'd in the viewless winds,

And blown with restless violence round about

The pendent world.

— *Measure for Measure*, Act III, Sc. 1

CONTENTS

THE LOCALE of this book is the Pacific Northwest, and a resident of Oregon or Washington will find much in it that is familiar to him. The characters, however, are imaginary, as are the situations, and the entire town of Cove; they do not represent, and are not intended to represent, actual persons, events or places.

—MURRAY MORGAN

THE VIEWLESS WINDS

— I —

THE INCIDENT

THE old man lurched through the fog. He careened against a lamppost, muttered "Scuse me," and reeled into the center of the street. He turned, swaying dangerously, and shouted, "Goddamit, I said I was sorry."

The WHOOM of the foghorn down by the bar answered him. He walked on, swearing to himself, his anger slowly dissolving into discomfort. The fog oozed through his plaid shirt; the wool smelled sour and clung to his chest. Drops of water formed on his heavy, waxed workpants but ran off without soaking through. His shoes, stiff from the salt of the beach, softened and squelched sullenly. He curled his toes against the cold.

He tried to remember why he had come to town, but his thoughts gravitated to the present. The fog filled him.

Earlier, before the fog rolled in off the Pacific, two lovers had parked their car on the beach road near the old man's shanty. When they went for a walk they left half of a fifth of Old Crow in the glove compartment of the Chev. And he had found it.

He lay on the long, yellow beach grass behind the silvery log and he drank the whiskey. Its fire spread through him; he giggled at the surprise of the couple who had lost their liquor, and then he thought of them, somewhere down the beach, and of what they might be doing. He stalked them through the drifted logs of the storm line and discovered them on a bed of moss cradled between the exposed roots of a cedar stump. He watched them, and their passion echoed within him. But when their desire was fulfilled and they lay in each other's arms, he felt hollow, let down. Spitefully he skittered the empty bottle across the sand toward them, and he ran away, panting and unpursued. Back in his cabin he thought of what he had seen. And his lust grew. He took three dollars in silver from a salmon can under a floorboard, tucked the money in his watchpocket, and started to town to visit Snug Haven, a whorehouse.

It was seven miles to town. The fog rolled in; the whiskey fire faded. Cold and exercise blunted his passion. Before he reached Cove, he was beyond thought. But not beyond feeling: sodden and bewildered, he walked on.

Another lamppost rushed toward him out of the mist. He threw up his hands to ward it off but his hands would not go where he wanted. The post slipped passed his guard. He mashed his face against the furrowed concrete.

He staggered back, his hard, big fists swinging wildly. He hit nothing more resistant than the fog, and at last he stopped. *Scared, huh? Scared uh me!* He buffed his knuckles on the palms of his hands, straightened until he tilted backwards, and paced away with dignity that degenerated into a stumble.

The hot pressure of the whiskey on his kidneys brought him to a stop. His stiff fingers fumbled at his fly, but before he was unbuttoned he heard footsteps. He jumped nervously. He remembered the sentence the police judge had dished out once for that—five days.

He veered into the protecting darkness of an alley. Behind him the sound of steps died away. *Couldn' fin' me. Couldn' catch me. Too smart for 'em.*

He leaned against a telephone pole and eased his kidneys and dreamed his favorite dream of his waking hours. He was walking the beach after a storm. It was raining, raining hard, and there was no one else on the beach. The tide was far out, so far that he was able to walk around the Point on the wet rocks below the cliff. Back against the cliff, wedged between smooth, sea-slimy slabs of shale, was a man's body. The legs pointed toward him, the hands and arms hung down the far side of the cleft. The man wore gray wool pants that clung to his thick, stiff legs and revealed the bulge of a wallet in his hip pocket. He reached in and took the dead man's wallet and put it inside his shirt and walked quickly back along the beach, the rain blowing past him. He saw no one, and no one saw him; the tide pulsed in, and the waves scoured away his footprints. There was a million dollars in the wallet.

The explosive barks of a terrier interrupted him before he could spend the million. There was a rush of feet, and the terrier materialized out of the mist, yapping frantically, but kept away by a chickenwire fence. The old man backed away, swearing. *Goddam dogs, wakin' everybody up middle uh the night.* Another dog took up the barking, then still another. In sudden panic the old man started to run. He scrambled over some debris between two garages and started across a backyard, sprinting stiffly.

A clothesline caught him across the forehead. He pawed the air to clutch at balance and his hands closed on a garbage can. For a moment he was anchored in a whirling world, then his weight pulled the can from its box. It fell with a metallic crash and he sprawled on top of it, sick from exertion.

An oblong of yellow appeared in the fog as a door opened. From above, a woman's voice, nervous, said, "Who is it? What's the matter?"

The old man pulled himself upright. "It's all ri', lady, Didn' mean nothin'."

Another light blossomed in the fog. He blinked up at the light. His head ached and his eyes burned. He was lying beside some porch steps. There was a lathwork grill under the porch and last year's vines clung to it. They looked like withered snakes.

"You're hurt. Your face is all bloody."

His numb fingers groped over his face. A little stab of pain knifed back from his mouth; he had split his lip against the lamppost. He sat up and looked at the woman; she bulked huge and menacing against the porch light. "I'm okay. Guy ran into me in the fog."

"With a car?" Her voice was sympathetic. Suddenly it seemed to him he had been hit by a car, left lying in the street. *Goddam hit-and-run bastards.* "Yeah," he said, starting—to his surprise—to cry. "Yeah. Hit me with his car. 'n when I wasn' lookin', either."

"I'll call a doctor."

Trapped. She'd trapped him. "No. No doctor." He knew now there had been no car. He would be found out. He would be caught lying, and they would laugh at him, and they'd say he was drunk and disorderly and he would be in jail again and the cops would laugh. *Goddam bastard cops.* He lurched to his feet and started to run, but he slipped in the wet ooze of garbage and went down. He lay there, sobbing, an old man in a world that took away his million dollars and threatened him with jail. and he felt sorry for himself.

He heard her feet on the steps, felt her helping hands under his arms. "No doctor," he muttered; "don't need no doctor, honest christ."

"You'll be all right."

"No doctor."

She steered him up the steps. The hot blast of house air almost turned his stomach. She maneuvered him onto a chair in the kitchen. He sat crying gently, his eyes shut. She drew water and washed his face; the warm cloth felt good and he stopped crying.

"Now let's look at you. Where are you hurt?"

His hand went to his mouth.

"I see that, but where else?"

He shook his head.

"You aren't hurt anywhere else?"

"Uh-uh."

"You weren't really hit by a car, were you?"

Already she had found out. She would laugh. He felt his cheeks bunch and his Adam's apple swell into a throat-choking knot.

"What really happened?" Her voice was still sympathetic. "Did you get into a fight?"

She didn't seem to care that he hadn't been hit by a car. He opened his eyes again and rubbed the tears off onto the side of his face, then forced his eyes into focus. She was not what she had seemed in the fog, huge and menacing; she was a small, brown-haired woman in a peppermint-striped dress.

"Somebody hit me in the fog," he said. "I didn' see him. He run away."

"That is a terrible thing to do," she said, no disbelief echoing in her voice. "I've seen you down by the ocean, haven't I? Don't you live in that sha— cabin near the Point?"

Suspicion flickered in him, dimly, then went out. "Yeah."

"That must be nice, living by the ocean. It's beautiful down there. We don't get over very much, any more."

He looked at her, wondering if she was making fun of him. She seemed serious.

"It's goddam cold all year. And I get hungry."

"Oh, I'm sorry," she said, as though it were her fault. "When did you eat last?"

"This morning. Clams," he lied. He'd had eggs and pancakes and thrown coffee, but he hungered for sympathy.

"You must be terribly hungry." She walked to the stove, a wood range, and lifted the lid from a pot. "There's some stew left. And coffee. Move your chair over to the table. I was warming it up for my husband." She glanced at him. "He's at a union meeting."

She brought him a thick plate with a thin stew and some bread. His stomach twisted at the sight of food, but he was afraid not to eat after saying he was hungry. He spooned the stew slowly to his mouth, not looking at her.

"Excuse me if I keep on ironing while you eat," she said. "Will promised to take me to a dance when he gets back, and I told him I'd press his suit."

He kept on eating. His stomach clenched and unclenched, and a pressure built up in his head until it felt like an over-heated tire. He put down the spoon and looked at her: Will's wife, somebody's wife, and he thought of the couple on the beach. She was humming "Night and Day" as she leaned forward over the ironing board. He watched the swing of her breasts inside the cotton dress as she moved the iron over the blue cloth. Glancing up, she caught his eyes on her.

"That's a funny iron," he said hurriedly.

"It's a steam iron. Will gave it to me for my birthday."

"Isn't it pretty big?"

"Oh, I'm strong." She knotted the muscle in her right arm and showed him. The gesture raised her breast and he could see the nipple under the stretched cloth. He thought of the beach. His mouth fell open and his breath rattled.

"I've got to finish this," she was saying rapidly. And then, more slowly, spacing the words and making them a little louder than necessary, "My husband is due any minute. He should be here any minute now."

He lurched to his feet. "Lemme help. I'll help you."

"No, thanks. I can do it. Have you had enough to eat?"

"Lemme help." He crossed to the ironing board. She kept on ironing, pressing down with short, determined strokes, not looking at him. The iron hissed over the serge.

She said, "Why don't you do the dishes instead?"

"I wanna iron. Don' you think I know how to iron, for cri' sake?"

"Of course you know how. It's only that I know exactly how Will wants it done."

"You can tell me how." He reached for the iron. His hand closed on her wrist. She tried to pull away. He held her. "You're not so strong." A fierce urge gripped him, and his jaws clamped together, and he repeated, through clenched teeth, "You're not so strong."

She wrenched her hand from under his, leaving him in possession of the iron. He leaned forward on the handle and stared at her across the ironing board."

"You're burning Will's coat."

"I just wanna help. That's all. Just wanna help."

"Give it back."

"You're not so strong."

She slapped him across the face, hard. "Get out of here, you old rummy."

He grabbed at her, knocking over the ironing board. She ducked under his arm toward the door, but, past him, behind him, with the door straight ahead, she tripped over the leg of the ironing board. He caught her shoulder with his left hand as she tried to get up. She clawed at his hand. "Let me go! Let me go! Let me go!"

Pain shot up his leg. He was clutching the iron in his right hand and it had seared his knee. Then her teeth sank into his forearm as she tried to make him let go of her shoulder.

He yelled and smashed her across the side of the head with the heel of the iron. She crumpled to the floor and lay still, face down on the flowered linoleum.

"Goddam iron burned my leg. Goddam iron." He dropped it, stepped over the woman's body, and shuffled through the door.

The fog closed round him.

— II —

THE NEWS

"You like it, huh, Gale?" the make-up man said. His inky hands moved over the half-filled form of page one.

"How'd you guess?"

"You got a poker face, the way Jane Russell's got a flat chest."

Gale Seward snapped his fingers with an extravagant gesture. "So that's why you win all my money." He hoisted a foot onto the proof press and, leaning forward on his knee, stared at the black, backward blocks that topped the next day's front page:

LABOR LEADER'S WIFE SLAIN

"Best story we've had in one hell of a time."

"Too bad some girl doesn't get murdered every day," the make-up man said.

Seward looked up. The printer was leaning forward over the make-up stone and his face was hidden by the cracked green eyeshade. "Was she a friend of yours?"

"I knew her in high school."

"Well, hell, Mac, I'm sorry she's dead, but . . ."

Seward paused, and the make-up man finished the sentence for him, saying sourly, ". . . but if she had to get killed, she couldn't have picked a better time for you."

"That's it," the city editor agreed; his tone was defensive and edged faintly with anger. Well, he thought, it *was* a wonderful time for a murder story to break. The body had been found at a quarter past eleven—ten minutes after the Cove radio station signed off its final news show; a full hour after the state edition of the *Oregonian* was locked up. The *Logger* had this story all to itself. "It's been a long time since we had a banner story the radio hadn't been kicking around all night," he told the make-up man.

MacIntyre, the one-legged printer who handled make-up, dropped some leads between paragraphs of the stories in column eight, then raised his head to meet the look he knew the city editor was leveling on him.

Mac liked Seward: they worked together each night, assembling from the gray blocks of the galleys a front page both coherent and lively, and they had for each other the respect of competent men whose work calls for cooperation but whose specialties are dissimilar enough to preclude rivalry. Mac's bitterness about the city editor's delight in the story had nothing to do with news values; it was more personal. As he had set the headline and fitted the story into the steel form, Mac had drifted back to his high school days, to the sweet, active spring of his junior year when he won a gold medal in the tri-county track meet and won, too, the favors of the golden-haired Finnish girl who later married Bull Dawson. The memory of that spring was delicate torment; for during the following summer he had taken a job in the deep woods, and one wet morning while riding to camp on a jerky log train, he had overestimated the spring in his long-muscled legs and dropped without screaming between the cars. The doctors had saved his life, but the accident cost him one of his hurdle-clipping legs; and it cost him, too, the favors of Delight Pelinen, who was too young and too pretty to stay in love with a cripple. In the alien loneliness of the crippled young, Mac hated her, then forgave her, almost; he never quite forgot her, even in the happiness of a good marriage, for she had been first and she had been in the days when he was whole. He could pass Dee on the sidewalk, or see her at the movies, or talk to her husband and never know a twinge of jealousy: but occasionally a memory pierced the armor of time and he ached for the spring when he was whole, and wholly in love.

"I didn't know Dee very well," he explained to Seward. "I just don't like to think of what's going to happen in this town if they don't nail the guy who killed her, but quick."

The foreman, a wiry, black-haired man of sixty-odd years, came over from the linotype with a stickful of corrections. The hot slugs smelled of acid, sour and pleasant. "Dawson did it," the foreman said, puffing the words out around the stem of a corncob pipe. "He killed her, sure as hell."

Seward gabled his eyebrows at the old man. The city editor's relations with the foreman were cool; the two sometimes quarreled about whether the editorial side or the backshop was responsible for overtime work and overset type. "Can I quote you, Mr. Thomas?"

The foreman tightened his lips and did not answer. He acted at being too busy inserting corrections in the page-one form to have time for argument.

The pressman waddled over. He was a fat, bald Irishman with tremendous shoulders and short, bowed legs. He picked up the sport-page form, braced it against his broad belt, and toddled off toward the flatbed press. "What Tommy means," he said, grunting each word because of the weight of the metal page, "is that he doesn't like Dawson." He lowered the page into place on the press and straightened up. "Tommy still thinks like a boss. That's all that's wrong with him. He'd be all right if he'd forget he used to own a paper. He might start thinking like a working stiff."

"You keep out of this," Thomas said without passion.

"Ah, take this and shove it." The pressman held up the wooden mallet with which he was tapping the sports page.

"I already have," said the foreman, pleased to have irritated the pressman. "Can't you tell?"

Gale Seward pulled the conversation back to its starting point. "You have any reason for thinking Bull killed her, Mr. Thomas? Any real reason?"

"The bastard's a Commie," Thomas said, tugging at the crank as he tightened the quoins on page two.

From inside the flatbed the pressman sounded a loud, "Ha!"

Thomas locked the type into place with an angry jerk of the crank. He took the pipe from his mouth and pointed the stem at the flatbed. "It's radicals like Dawson are ruining the trade-union movement. They cost us the respect of the people. Time was when they'd have ridden Bull Dawson out of town on a rail."

"Time was when they burned witches."

"Now look here, dammit, don't go implying I'm not a good union man. I'm all for *good* unions."

"Yeah, but for you the only good union is a dead union."

MacIntyre kicked a tall iron wastebasket with his wooden leg and yelled, "Bell, bell. End of the round. Break it up, you guys." He shoved his cracked eyeshade back on top of his curly hair and wiped his forehead with the back of his hand, leaving an inky streak from temple to temple. "That's what I don't like about this business," he said to Seward. "Everybody's going to get sore as hell about this murder. It'll split the town seven ways from Sunday." He leaned forward and flicked a speck of shiny lead off the inky block of the first letter in the bannerline. "Everyone in town who hates Bull for one thing or another is going to think he killed her."

Thomas said bitterly, "And every son of a bitching Red in town will say Bull didn't, even after they burn him."

Seward thought, *What a swell story.* "I see what you mean," he said to MacIntyre. And then to Thomas, "They don't burn people in this state, they hang 'em. Anyway, Bull didn't knock her off."

Thomas glanced at him. "No?"

"No." Seward tapped the ink-blackened engraving set in columns five and six of page one. He twisted his head so the light was right on the picture, a shot of a blonde in a two-piece suit. Her hands were clasped behind her head and her hips rested against a log in a way that pushed her pelvis forward. "Christ, man, just look at that! It's enough to give a eunuch ennui. If you had something like that lying around the house, would you conk it with a flat iron?"

"Tommy doesn't even remember what you can do with a matched set like that," the pressman said. "The last picture that roused the beast in him was *'September Morn.'*"

To Seward, the picture was one of the best things about the story. The *Logger* had no engraving plant, and he seldom found an engraving suitable for a local story in the filing cabinet behind the files of back copies. "I don't remember this cut at all, Mac. Where did we get it?"

"Came in while you were in the army. Chamber of commerce publicity. Her suit is made out of clamshells from down by the point. The boss never used it. Thought Dee was too naked."

Seward grinned, "Just think of that. *Too* naked. With a build like that." He shook his head. "Just goes to show how wrong the boss can be."

The make-up man finished locking up page one. The pressman came over and lugged it to the flatbed. Thomas turned off his linotype and it ran down with a diminuendo of ticks and clacks. Seward went through the swinging door to the front office and ran through his end-of-shift routine: he phoned the hospital and police station to make sure no catastrophe had occurred in the last hour, turned off the news association teletype, and settled down to read copy on the next day's syndicated political column.

The *Logger* was a small paper. It claimed a circulation of 8,000 and had a press run of 4,900—not all of which sold. There were about 400 inches of ads daily, except on Fridays, when the total was over 700 and the sheet was tight.

A four-man staff turned out the news. Seward was called city editor but performed the duties of managing editor and wire editor as well. The other staffers were Helene Lewis, the society editor; Frank Velecich, sports editor and proof-reader; and Joe Kalinen, reporter.

The boss, Rutherford B. Olson, was a superannuated politician, a former congressman. He wrote the editorials, or at least clipped them from other papers, and, every year or so, had bursts of energy during which he composed long stories stuffed with implausible statistics purporting to show that new industries were about to crowd in upon Cove to supplement its lumber-and-fish economy. When the Boss was not being energetic, Seward had the paper pretty much to himself.

At the age of twenty-nine, Seward had bracketed five years of newspaper work around a three-year hitch in the army—an interruption he had hated every second of. He had come to Cove straight from the University of Missouri School of Journalism, answering an ad in *Editor and Publisher*. He started as a reporter—*the* reporter—and within a year graduated to sports editor; after pasturing in that pleasant field of alliterative nicknames and self-awarded by-lines, he had been almost reluctant to accept the city editorship—but he had never regretted moving up. He loved the *Logger* and felt possessive about it. He fretted over make-up, sweated over the way to cram the day's news budget into eight pages (he resented every inch taken up by advertising even more than he resented the space wasted on women's fashions). He worked sixty hours a week trying to make the *Logger* what he thought a small-town paper should be, and each week he signed a slip saying he had worked forty hours. When the day's work was over he would spread the paper on the floor of his hotel room and study the make-up. Then he would re-read every local story, looking for follow-up angles. He would check the wire stories for local implications. And when he went to bed, around four A.M., he often had nightmares about misspelled names in headlines.

For Cove, as a town, he cared little. His attitude toward Cove was that of a mason for the quarry that supplies his stone. He did not identify himself with the town, but he weighed the stories on the scales of local interest. He played up news of lumber and fish, of Finland and Yugoslavia, of Lutherans and Catholics. But that was as mechanical as thinking in headline units, and he often found himself framing everyday thoughts in words that would fit into the *Logger* head schedule:

SET THE ALARM
FOR EIGHT A.M.
or
PLEASE GIVE ME
A HAM SANDWICH

His civic detachment was involuntary. On arriving in Cove he had consciously tried to become part of the community. He had joined the Elks and the Eagles; he had dated the local girls; he had cultivated the old-timers. But social life was too much work for a man whose job started in the afternoon and ended at two A.M.; and he loved the paper, while he only liked the Cove girls. After getting out of the army, he had been satisfied with acquaintances rather than friends. He was not lonely: the paper was enough.

Though he had known Dee Dawson slightly and was well acquainted with her husband, Seward did not think of the murder in terms of people: he reacted completely to news values. He thought of Dee not as a human being but, instead, as a Murdered Beauty, the sex angle in a swell story. And the fact that she was Bull's wife was just pure gravy; for Bull Dawson was controversial, and controversy could lift any story out of the ruck.

In the backshop the flatbed creaked into action, rattling the partition between front and back shops. The press ran for a minute or two, then stopped. The pressman waddled in with damp copies that smelled wetly of ink. Seward read the story of the murder. He had written it himself, from facts phoned in by Joe Kalinen, who had picked them up at the police station after Dawson phoned the cops to say he'd found his wife's body in the kitchen.

It had been a good story to write; but rereading it, he wished he'd had more time (he always wished that the first time he went over a story written under deadline pressure) and he wished, too, that he had been able to go over to the Dawson house to look for the little details that add color; but it had been too near the deadline and the boss had been screaming like an eagle lately whenever there were overtime charges. So he had just batted the story out from the dope Kalinen phoned in. But now he would go over to the house to get stuff for the next day's piece. He'd told Kalinen to go, but Kalinen was hopeless on color.

Seward ran through the paper quickly, checking to see that the headlines were right side up, that the page datelines had been brought forward from yesterday, that the captions matched the pictures below them. He stuck his head through the backshop door, yelled "Let 'er go," and, taking his coat, left the office.

The fog lay heavy on the town. Down the street from the

Logger plant, the neon light over the Greek's made a bloody splotch on the gray blanket. The street lights were yellow and dim. It took Seward half an hour to walk the twelve blocks that carried him across the heart of town and into the Lower Hill section where Bull lived and Dee had died.

The Dawson house was a small frame building in the middle of a block of small frame buildings. All the houses in the Lower Hill section had been thrown together during the mid-twenties, just before the crash; through the thirties the mill workers who had bought them were so busy trying to meet payments that they had no chance to make repairs; in the first half of the forties there was the priority business that nobody could beat; and after the war ended materials were either unavailable, or for millionaires only. Even in the softening fog, the houses looked bleak and shabby. They had seen a heap of living and it had left them unhomelike.

Lights glowed in the windows at Dawson's. A knot of spectators, most of them men, stood on the soggy parking and stared at the windows. Seward recognized Andy Lazarevich, a tall Croat with a great Slavic nose. Andy ran a wholesale grocery business that supplied rations for all the purse seine boats owned by local Slavs. He usually draped his Abe Lincoln frame in funereal black, but at the moment he wore a brown raincoat over a pink-and-blue flannel nightgown; his size-twelve feet were encased in snout-nosed slippers from the old country. Andy nodded a greeting, a solemn greeting, and rumbled in a voice that seemed to start from around his knees, "This is a terrible thing, Mr. Seward."

"Terrible," Seward acknowledged. "Is Bull inside?"

"No, Mr. Seward." Andy used Mister for everybody except Slavs. (Slavs he divided into Croatians, whom he called Brother; Poles, whom he called by their first names, and Serbs, whom he would not speak to. "I think it is only Mr. Policeman Haarka in the house."

"Where's Bull?"

Andy shrugged.

Seward went up the steps. The porch was glassed in against the winter-long rains that fell on Cove. He tried the porch door and it opened. The porch was filled with flower pots and long boxes from which hung strands of yellow ferns. The inner door was locked. He knocked, and the door was opened by a slender, yellow-haired man in police uniform, Warren Haarka, a patrolman.

"Hi, Gale, come on in. Your boy Kalinen just flagged ass out of here."

"Thanks." Seward went into the living room, a square room crowded with overstuffed furniture and decorated with prints of flowers. "Bull around?"

The patrolman shook his head and eased himself onto the worn couch. He stretched, revolving his elbows slowly and stiffening his legs so that his heels left the floor. "Bull went with the chief," he said around a yawn. His heels banged down onto the carpet. "Goddam, but I'm sleepy. Haven't had my coffee yet."

"Why don't you make some?"

Haarka looked from Seward to the kitchen door. "In there? Christ, man, there's still blood on the floor!"

Seward walked to the door and looked in. The kitchen seemed like any other kitchen he had seen in Cove. The paint was old but the gadgets were new: a wall can-opener; a double hotplate with built-in toaster that sat on the shelf above the wood range. The ironing board had been picked up and Dawson's suit was folded, clumsily, on top of it. The spindly pine legs of the ironing board straddled a smudge of blood, already browning.

"Where's the iron?"

"The Chief took it."

"Any fingerprints?"

"Jesus H., yes. The whole damn town. When Bull found her, he went running out in the street, yelling bloody murder, and before hell's half minute the whole damn neighborhood was in here. Christ on a crutch, Gale, but we must have got fifty million fingerprints, all different."

"Any idea who did it?"

"Christ only knows." Haarka yawned again and stretched extravagantly. "Jesus god, but I could use some coffee. This night trick is a bitch."

"I'll look after the place if you want to whip up to the Greek's for a quick one."

"The Chief'd chew my ass clear off." Haarka grinned and hoisted himself out of the soft upholstery. "But what the hell? Just don't let anybody in."

"What about Dawson if he comes back?"

"Hell, yes, let him in. Man's home's his castle, always say. But sorta keep an eye on him." Haarka took his white policeman's slicker and chauffeur cap from the deer-horn coathanger by the door and left, closing the door quietly.

Gale wandered around the house. It would be distinguished as The Murder House for some time, he supposed, but it was just another house. Nothing special. Its commonness depressed him. No furnishings that would add color to the story; and it takes so many more words to describe an ordinary thing than a strange one. He looked into the bedroom: double bed, dresser covered with cosmetic jars and photos of Bull and Dee (Why, he wondered, do people who see each other daily put formal pictures of each other on the dresser?), Bull's pajamas draped over the closet doorknob, a collection of shoes and slippers scattered about the floor.

He looked in the bathroom, a routine layout that smelled of Clorox. Walking back across the bedroom to the living room, he glanced at the pictures again and wondered if he should steal them; stealing photos was a journalistic habit he had not acquired, but this was due less to moral scruples than to the fact that the *Logger* had no photoengraving plant. He went to the dresser and started to pry the nails from the back of the ten-cent-store frame around Dee's picture.

Something moved in the next room—in the kitchen.

The sound was the scuffle of a foot on the linoleum. He held his breath. There was a rustle of cloth.

He was scared. He was not superstitious, but he was scared of the sound that came from the kitchen. His stomach knotted and his knees went soft, but he forced himself to walk toward the room the girl had been killed in, the room the sounds now came from. He hesitated a moment at the door, then swung it open.

A woman stood beside the ironing board. Her back was to Seward. She was tall. She wore a red raincoat that was shiny with moisture. A white scarf, pulled tight over her head, did not completely confine her brown hair.

"Looking for something?" His voice sounded loud and strange, the way it had the time he'd talked over the PA system at the ball park.

She started violently, gasped, turned toward him. He had an impression of high cheekbones, of a long nose, of dark eyes, a flash of teeth. Then she was running. He followed her through the back door, which stood open, and for a few steps across the yard. But she faded from sight in the fog and he did not follow.

Haarka came back a few minutes later, sweating from three cups of hot coffee and a five-block run in his raincoat. Seward told him about the girl.

"Forget it," the patrolman said. "Jesus H., don't worry about it. She must have been just another bitch-bastard thrill seeker. Holy Christ, the place has been crawling with them all night."

"Okay," Seward agreed. "We don't even tell the Chief, that right?"

Haarka's thin face creased in a grin. "That's what I always say. Jesus god, yes. What the Chief don't know won't hurt me."

Seward walked back through the fog to the office, picked up several copies of the paper, and went a block and a half down Elm Street to the police station.

The cops were housed in the basement of the city hall, an ugly building of monolithic concrete, three times too big for the town. Mayor Everett, who was primarily responsible for its construction, had a stock explanation for its size: "The main function of a town hall is to look good on postcards." The building had a front door, but scavenger hunters stole so many cuspidors from the council room that the door was locked at five-ten in the evening, usually by the assistant city treasurer on her way home. So Seward went around to the alley entrance to call on the cops.

The Number Two prowl car was sitting in the parking area, empty but with its lights on and motor humming. He honked the horn, just for the hell of it, and ran down the steps into the station.

Three men stood in front of the booking desk, talking. Two were huge hulks, over six feet tall, broad-shouldered, broad-faced, square-chinned—the prowl-car crew. The third man was Chief of Police Roger Snow, a compact, handsome man in brown tweeds.

Behind the booking desk the night desk sergeant was asleep, his visored cap tilted over his face, his heels braced against the molding of the radio booth door. In the far corner of the big room another large cop, still wearing his wet slicker-cape, leaned against the wall and munched on a sandwich.

The prowler pair said, "Hi." The Chief said, "How's

tricks?" The night sergeant snored gently. Bill Elliott, the sergeant eating the sandwich, kept on eating it. Seward told the Chief tricks were fine; said "Not bad" to the prowler boys; and asked Elliott, "How are the whores?"

"Peaceful, and you can dot the A."

Elliott was the oldest man on the force in point of service. He had quarreled with the Chief and was pounding a night beat that took in the town's three remaining whorehouses— Snug Harbor, Easy Rooms, and New Deal. His exchange with Seward was a nocturnal ritual they punctiliously observed, though neither found the joke funny.

Seward passed out the papers he had brought, then turned to Snow. "Whodunnit, Chief?"

Snow tilted his head and pointed his chin at Seward as though it might be loaded. "Done what?"

"Killed her."

"Who do you think?"

"Suicide."

The Chief laughed. He was as amused as if his arm had been twisted. "Ha ha. Suicide. That's good."

"Got any ideas?"

"Lots of ideas."

"Clues?"

"We found a body."

Jenssen, the taller of the prowl-car officers, said, "Damn nice body, too. I'd like to have been digging some of that stuff."

"Who wouldn't?" said Andreason, the other prowler.

"Who wasn't?" Snow put in.

"Seriously, Chief, who do you figure did it?"

Snow drew a bead on Seward with his chin again. "How the hell would I know? This is the second murder we've had in six years. I'm no goddam gumshoe. My job's keeping cars from going too fast and high school kids from tearing off too much. For the lousy dough this burg pays you don't get Sherlock Holmes."

"When do you expect an arrest?"

"When we find somebody to arrest."

From the far corner boomed the voice of Elliott unexpectedly. "Regardless of whether that somebody killed her?"

Snow spun around. "Now listen, you. . . ."

"Say it, Chief, say it. I'd love to hear you say it in front of a reporter."

"You're goddam right I'll say it. What the goddam hell you mean, Regardless of if he killed her? You're too goddam smart, Elliott, too goddam smart for your own good. One of these days. . ."

He walked toward the cop. The sound of his heels on the linoleum rang in the big, bare room. The prowl-car men shifted their feet in embarrassment at the quarrel. Elliott leaned away from the wall and straightened until he loomed half a head above the Chief; he balanced forward on the balls of his feet and he moved his shoulders slightly from side to side; he kept opening and closing his large, rather soft, hands, opening and closing them slowly, deliberately. He looked like a she–bear in the spring—still sleepy, but powerful and dangerous and probably mean.

"Go on, Chief, go on. I love to listen to you. Let's hear about where the prowler was between nine and eleven."

The prowler pair stopped shifting their feet. "Now listen here, Bill," Jenssen began, but Snow shut him off with an impatient downward gesture of his left hand. In evenly spaced words Snow said, "The prowler was out on the High Road looking for some kids who'd been seen going into the bushes with a blanket."

"The High Road is outside town."

"You know goddam good and well we go outside town

when we get reports like that. If some girl is getting laid, her folks get just as sore if it's outa town as in town."

"Who reported seeing the kids?"

"Somebody phoned it in."

"There's no slip on the file about it."

"The hell there isn't. I made it out myself." Snow's voice rose to a shout. Elliott smiled down at him. The Chief, his anger compounded by the realization he had lost his temper first, opened his mouth twice, said nothing, then shrugged stiffly, turned and said, "Civil Service." He used the words as if they totaled eight letters. He stomped into his office and slammed the door.

The prowler pair looked from the closed door to Elliott several times, swinging their gaze back and forth simultaneously, like spectators at a tennis match. Finally Jennsen said, "Lord, Bill, you're just asking for punishment. He'll have you flattening your feet till hell won't have it."

Elliott stuck out his lower lip and sucked on the upper. He cocked his head sideways and slanted a long look at his fellow cops. He lit a cigarette, taking his time, and huffed jets of smoke through his nose. Finally he said, "Screw you, too."

"Okay, sorehead," Andreason said. "We warned you." The prowler pair slid into their raincoats and went out. Jenssen tried to slam the door, but it was on an air spring and closed gently.

Seward stared at Elliott, a stare that asked a question. The big cop suddenly grinned, shook his head, and sat down on the police judge's desk; he took another sandwich from a paper sack: Seward's move. Seward stepped to the booking desk, leaned over and picked up the spindle from the shelf by the telephone. On the spindle were blue slips listing the calls that had come in since eight P.M., when the night ser-

geant came on duty. The top one said, "Dee D. dead." The
rest were the usual stuff: a dead cat to be picked up, a fight
in a beer parlor, a complaint by a sleepy citizen about a noisy
neighbor, a schoolteacher's report that a man was beating his
wife, a report that small boys were throwing stones at a
street light. A busy night—but no kids in the bushes on the
High Road. He put the spindle back in place.

"What's it all about?" he asked Elliott.

Elliott stood up. His heavy face was impassive. "Ask the
Chief." He buttoned his rain cape. "It'd make quite a story."
He went out.

Seward knocked on the door to the Chief's office and was
told to come in. The office was small, neat, windowless; it
might have been a cell. The furniture was simple: a heavy
metal desk, four metal folding chairs, and a metal filing
cabinet. Seward hated the room, had hated it for seven years
—ever since he watched two cops work over a man they suspected of stealing tires. (The man confessed, and his confession broke up a state-wide tire-stealing, gas-siphoning gang.)
But Seward could still remember the sounds he had made
when the hose slapped into the raw palm of his hand.

"What's the pitch, Chief?"

"With Elliott?"

"Yeah."

"Oh, the crazy bastard thinks he ought to be chief or
something. Always telling me how to run the station. He was
like that before the war, but now that he's come back a hero
he figures he's got me by the balls. His father-in-law is on
the council, and he's a Civil Service rating, and he's got that
you-can't-fire-a-vet business. He's trying to make me can him,
and if I do he'll kick up a big stink and make a political
issue of it, and try to get himself made Chief."

"But what about the prowl car?"

"None of your Goddam . . ." Snow brought himself up

sharply. "Sorry, fella, didn't mean to flip my lid. It's been quite a night."

"That's all right. What about the prowler?"

"Oh, I sent the boys out on that report about the kids on the High Road. The car went out of the city all right, but we do that all the time. You know how it is. If some alleged virgin is getting climbed, we figure it's our business to stop it, city limits or no city limits, because if she gets knocked up she may not remember whether she was in town or not the night she forgot to be careful, and her parents will raise hell with me. So I sent the prowler out, and that sorehead noticed it was out of town at the time the Dawson gal got killed. He thinks he can make something of it."

"Can he?"

"Hell, no. But it's the kind of business that gripes my guts, is all." He gazed gloomily at the dull green top of his desk. "Oh, Jesus, yes, he can give me a rough ride on it if we don't nail the guy who killed her. Every union in town is going to be bleating their brains out about Bull's old lady getting killed." He shook his head and grinned ruefully. "Son of a bitch. Isn't that the way it always goes? Politics."

He pulled open the top drawer of his desk and took out a piece of paper, which he handed to Seward. It was a note saying, "Kids on High Road. RS."

Snow said, "I took the call in here and forgot to put this on the spindle."

"I see." The note was in pencil. Seward wished it were ink so he could see if it would still smear. "What do you really think of Mrs. Dawson, Chief? Off the record."

Snow said, "Well, from all accounts she was tossing it around plenty. Maybe somebody got jealous?"

"Bull?"

Snow raised his shoulders and spread his hands. "I don't mean anybody. I had quite a talk with Bull tonight. It looks like he's air-tight. He was at a union meeting all evening until he came back and found her dead. He's got a million guys who saw him at the meeting; at least, he says he has—we have to check on it, but he wouldn't be enough of a dope to lie about something like that. She was getting stiff so she was probably dead at least an hour when we got there. That's about all we know."

"But you think Bull did it?"

"Jesus, fella, I said I didn't know. I wouldn't mind pinning it on that bastard. He gripes my guts. But I don't know. But, hell, when a gal is putting out to half the population, it's only natural to wonder about her husband if she's found dead."

"Can I quote you?" Seward asked, smiling.

"Hell, no. Far as we're concerned, she was a double-sealed virgin—no disrespect meant to Bull. There's no immorality in this fair city. You know that."

"You going to try checking up on all her lovers?"

"Now there's a job. It'd be like taking census. But if nothing else breaks, I suppose we'll have to."

"Anything likely to pop tonight?"

Snow shook his head. "I'll phone you if it does."

"Okay, thanks."

Snow stood up and looked squarely into the newspaper-man's eyes. "Don't let anyone sell you a bill of goods on this."

"Elliott?"

"I don't mean anybody in particular. Just a manner of speaking." Snow smiled and looked as blank and pleasant as any lantern-jawed 180-pounder who hadn't shaved for eighteen hours could look at two-thirty A.M. in a police station.

"Don't worry. I'm not accepting any fibrous pfennigs."

Seward left the office. He took a piece of copy paper from his pocket, wrote "BOO" on it, and, going behind the booking desk, put the paper on the lap of the sleeping night sergeant. On the way out he looked at the radio log. No one had reported sending a call to the prowler to go to High Road and check on kids in the bushes.

Walking down to the Greek's, Seward churned the incidents around in his mind. They didn't make sense, and he shoved them aside. He'd puzzle them out later. He began to think of the phrases he'd use in the Dawson story tomorrow but his thoughts slid off the subject, and for the last block to the cafe he tried to guess how L'il Abner would avoid Daisy Mae, come Sadie Hawkins Day.

The Greek's place was empty except for the waitress and Nellie. The waitress was a new girl in town, and Nellie was established at Snug Harbor. The waitress had on too much rouge, too much lipstick, and some nail polish that made her look as if she'd caught her fingers in a door. She watched Nellie drink coffee and her expression indicated she found the performance indecent. Nellie wore a neat blue suit, her hair was brushed, and she had on only an elementary amount of make-up. She was a little drunk. She held the big coffee cup in both hands and she sipped carefully over the thick rim.

As Gale Seward sat down two stools away, Nellie turned to him. "The old goat bit me," she said. "Imagine that. All this time and I still let an old goat bite me."

"Where?"

"Where do you think." It was no question.

"That's bad."

"Darn right it's bad. Girls get cancer that way. It's very bad. I said to him, 'Lissen, you, this isn't that kind of a house. You wanna bite ladies, you go somewhere else.' I told him."

The waitress plonked a glass of water on the counter in front of Seward. She made a swipe across the greasy plastic surface with a greasier rag and asked, "Wassitgonnabe?" In a whisper that wouldn't carry much beyond British Columbia, she added, "If she's bothering you, Mister. . ."

"Coffee and a hamburger san. That's all."

The waitress flounced heavily away and buried her discolored nails in a mound of hamburger. "A lady," said the whore, softly, "a real lady. Thanks for sticking up for me, champ."

"A pleasure."

"Guess I talk too much. But imagine an old hand like me getting bit."

"They tell me even Joe Louis doesn't always remember to cover up in the clinches. Besides, you aren't so awfully old."

"Twenty-eight," she lied. Seward had looked over the cops' files on local prostitutes and knew she was in her mid-thirties. "But sometimes I feel awful old. Really I do. Sometimes I feel so old I just don't care." She stared at the bottom of her coffee cup. Seward thought she might cry.

"It's a rough go," he said.

"It's not so bad, really. There's dough in it, and it's honest." She waited for him to argue, but he didn't. "It's just so damn monotonous. Same thing, over and over. Guy told me a story tonight. Said he picked it up in Alaska. Seems a fella went into a fancy house in Fairbanks and asked the boss-lady for a real nice girl. So she got him a real nice girl who wouldn't let him touch her. Jeez, but that would be fun."

"Suppose so."

Nellie stood up, checked her looks in a mirror, and laid a quarter on the counter. "Darned if I don't feel like spending a night in a hotel," she said. "But they probably wouldn't give me a room, alone. I'm only good enough for them when they want to send me up to some traveling salesman." She stood by Seward's stool and put a hand on his arm, then took it away, self-consciously. "Thanks, champ. I needed someone to talk to. You get sort of sick of the girls and the trade."

"Suppose so," Seward said again. He was getting bored. He was tired and it had been a long day.

"You work nights?"

"Yeah."

"All the best people work nights. You drive truck?"

"I'm a newspaper man."

"No foolin'. Kinda guy who's got to call it a house of ill repute, huh? I used to know a lot of newspaper guys in San Francisco."

"That I don't doubt."

She laughed. "Well, so long, champ. Maybe someday I'll have a story for you."

"I'll hold my breath."

"You do that little thing."

She left, and the waitress came down from the grill, carrying a cup of coffee, not all of which was in the saucer, and a lump of half-raw hamburger between two cold buns.

"You know who that was?" she asked, her voice raspy with indignation.

"Sure. Don't you?"

"I must say some folks aren't very choosey."

The only answer he could think of for that was nasty, so he let it ride. The waitress retreated to the far end of the counter, hitched her girdle, and went to work on her make-up. Seward nursed the coffee along as far as it would go, read the paper over again, found a typo in a society-page headline, gave up, and walked to his hotel, a block away.

Outside his door, he realized someone was in the room. Light seeped through the crack, and he could hear the leather creak in his reading chair. The night's events had left him jittery; it took all his courage to open the door.

Bill Elliott looked up from a copy of *Time*. "I just barged in," the big cop said. "I got tired of hanging around in the corridor. Didn't think you'd mind."

"It's all right." He took off his coat and hung it up. "You scared the living hell right out of me, Bill."

"Sorry. But I wanted to talk to you."

"Okay by me." Seward took a gallon jug of claret from under his bed, hoisted it over his crooked elbow, and poured two water glasses full. He set the jug on the seat of a straight-backed chair, kicked off his shoes without unlacing them, and flopped on the bed, leaning back on his elbows. "All right, shoot."

"What are the chances of the *Logger's* starting a campaign to get rid of Snow as Chief?"

"On what grounds?"

"Incompetence and crookedness and favoritism."

"Where's the proof?"

"I'll tell you all I know. And it's plenty."

"Any documentary proof?"

"No, but after I blow things wide open, the grand jury could probably dig up all it needs."

"No dice."

Elliott sighed heavily.

"Look, Bill, anything we run we have to be able to prove or we're wide open for libel. That's point A. Point B is that the boss writes the editorials, or lifts them from other papers. And the only things he'll take a stand against are sin, sodomy and the Soviet Union. And Democrats in season. Hell, you know that."

Elliott stared sullenly into the bottom of his glass. He turned it so the grainy red drops gathered in a tiny pool, then tossed them down. Unsmiling, he reached for the jug, filled his glass, emptied it in one long draw, hunched his shoulders in a shudder.

"I'm going to make a speech," he declared. "Even if you don't print it, you damn well ought to know it. This town stinks, Gale, stinks till hell won't have it."

"Surprise, surprise."

Elliott's broad mouth twisted into a faint grin. "Right you are—that's not news. But I don't mean the little grafts, like protection from whores and cuts from the pinball operators. That's graft, and it's wrong; but what the hell, there's always going to be some of that. What corks me is this gestapo business."

As he spoke, Elliott's pale eyes were focused on Seward. "All right, smile, goddamit. I'm being melodramatic. Sure. But when I say gestapo, I damn well mean gestapo and there's no call for you to get a silly, superior grin on your puss. The trouble with you newspaper guys is you spend so much time acting cynical you haven't time to learn what there is to be cynical about."

Seward said, "The editorial page always bores me. Let's have the news."

"Sure. Sure. Facts. Now here's what I mean about gestapo. The smartest thing the fascists ever did was realize people are bigger bastards than they want known. Put a tail on any man, keep him there, and he'll turn up something that guy doesn't want made public. Hitler knew that. For tough guys, the fanatics, the strong ones, the Nazis used concentration camps and goon squads; but for the average guy, the little businessman, the well-meaning little liberal without a lot of guts, all they needed was the name of his mistress. Anything he didn't want known. Anything he was ashamed of.

"All right. That was the gestapo, and we don't have any, you say. The hell we don't. We've got half a dozen agencies that spend their time spying on private citizens. Some of them work for Congress, some for Justice, some for the military. But they build up dossiers on private citizens, and I'd just as soon trust the Army or some of those bastards in Congress with the atom bomb as I would with those files."

Seward said, "So what, as long as they don't blackmail people with them?"

"Look, pal, the dope in those dossiers has a nasty habit of turning up at election time. Right now it's used against left wingers, but that doesn't mean it couldn't be used against anybody else. Remember how it was during the Russo-Finnish war, the first half of it, that is, when it was still Poor Little Finland?

"You know a hell of a lot of the Finns around here are in the country illegally. Trade-union people who had to get out of Finland, but quick, when Mannerheim first took over and was knocking off labor leaders. Their relatives smuggled them in here in fishing boats, and they've been here ever since. Twenty years. Long enough to raise families. Then boom—comes the war over there and people here get steamed up and our government steps in, arrests half a dozen of them and boots them clear the hell back to Finland. Why? Christ only knows. That's the sort of thing happens when there are dossiers lying around where the bastards can get hold of them."

"The government had a right to check up on them."

"Oh, sure. And it had a right to do all the checking it did on everybody and his brother during the war, too. People were investigated from hell to breakfast. Down at the station we supplied info' on half the people in Cove to half the other people. Jesus Christ, they know which of the local businessmen go to which whorehouses, and they know which schoolteachers we sort of keep an eye on about little girls, and they know more about you than you do yourself. I'll bet you don't know what your laundry mark is: well, they know it."

Elliott filled his glass a third time and took a mouthful of wine, then wiped his lips with the back of his hand.

"That's the national picture, and I know there's not one damn thing you can do about it. In a time of atom bombs you sure as hell aren't going to talk the country out of the FBI or Army Intelligence, just because the files are a threat. But locally—"

Seward interrupted. "You mean we have a local spy organization?"

"Wheels within wheels," said Elliott, emptying his glass again. "This spy stuff is contagious as all hell. The Chief has a wonderful file on all the city politicos, no kidding. There's one councilman goes on a Peeping Tom tear about once a year, and another who—well, never mind what. We've run them in, and the Chief lets them go. But after he lets them go they damn well vote right on police pay raises and things like that. But hell, that sort of thing's not exactly new. What should interest you are the new twists, you being a newspaper man. You know Steve Barovich?"

"By sight."

"How about by reputation?"

"I think he lost the Thanksgiving Day game with a fumble or something, one year. That was back before my time, but it keeps coming up every Thanksgiving. He's working at the plywood plant now, isn't he?"

"In a manner of speaking. You don't know what he does nights?"

"He's a good-looking guy. I can imagine."

"Well, guess again, evil mind. For the last four months Steve Barovich has been gathering information about local labor leaders. He's been trying to get stuff to prove they're communists and, failing that, to dig up dirt on their private lives."

"So what? There've always been labor spies. It's just one part of the picture. What about goon squads?"

Elliott huffed a sigh. "All right. There have always been

spies. Now listen, dammit. Steve Barovich was hired by the Promote Prosperity League to get the dirt on the local labor boys. About a month ago I caught him going through the window at the Fish Packers Union and ran him in for breaking and entering. Well, to make a long story not so long, he made a deal with the chief. Steve was released. So he tells the Chief what he finds about the labor boys as well as telling the League. He also tells the Chief what assignments he gets and who gave them to him. And to make things just ducky, whenever Steve is going to break into somebody's place, the Chief makes sure none of us will be around to interfere. He sends the prowl car off on a wild-goose chase. Tonight. . ."

Seward sat up on the bed. "Holy God. Tonight he sent the prowler. . ."

"Tonight the prowler was sent away from the Lower Hill. My hunch is that tonight Steve was going to break into Bull Dawson's house."

Seward got off the bed and stood for nearly a minute looking down at Elliott, who turned the water glass in his big, soft hands. Seward found himself thinking of Elliott, rather than of what Elliott had said. He walked to the window and looked out at the fog, now pearled by the rising sun. "If Snow gets the heave-ho, what does that make you?"

"Chief, maybe." When Seward turned around, Elliott met his gaze squarely. "I wouldn't mind being Chief. But that's not what I want most. I just hate to see bastards get decent people by the balls."

"How much of this can you prove?"

"Not much, unless we can get at the books and the files in the Chief's office."

Seward started pacing the floor. "We can't print it unless we can prove it; or unless the charges are made in an official document, so that it can be published without our having proof."

"I'll swear out an affidavit."

"No, that doesn't do it. If we ran an affidavit, we'd assume responsibility for the truth of the affidavit. An official document has to be connected with some public proceeding. If we ran it on your say-so, and couldn't prove what you said, the Chief would have himself a newspaper as soon as the libel suit was over."

"But if it got published, there'd be a big hullaballo and an investigation and then we could get at the files and prove the charges."

"Christ, man, it's not my paper. I can't go gambling another man's paper on a hunch that things would work out right."

Seward sat down on the bed and stared at the carpet. After a time, he said, "What we need is to get the charges part of an official record."

"How about council meeting next week? Would that do it? They're going to take up the petition for more money for city employees. What if I get up to testify and instead of saying I want ten bucks more a week, make a speech saying the Chief is accessory to a murder?"

"I think that would do it. I think that would be fine."

"I'll think it over, then. It would cost me my job." Elliott stood up. "I'd better be taking off. I'm still on duty and I've already missed two calls. Thanks for the drinks."

"Thanks for the information." Seward walked with him to the door. "When will you let me know?"

"Day after tomorrow. Or sooner. 'Night."

"Or good morning."

Elliott walked down the hall, his metaled heels sounding loud between the narrow walls, his holstered Colt wagging on his hip.

It was after five. Gale Seward went to bed and fell asleep at once. He dreamed of a girl in a red slicker, a girl with high cheekbones and gleaming white teeth, the girl he had surprised in Dawson's kitchen.

— III —

MORNING

EVERY morning Herman Peterson looked down on the town, his town. He had a fine view of it, the best there was, and that seemed fitting for him, for Old Herm—as Peterson usually thought of himself—had built the place, lock, stock and sawmill.

When Peterson first came to the cove, cruising timber, there were a few cabins and a clearing where the Indians camped when salmon were running in the Tala River. He could remember the first time he had climbed Siwash Point and stood between the boles of the ancient spruce, and looked down on the brown river that curved across the flats of Tala Valley and disappeared in the mile-wide cove.

He thought of it again this morning as he rolled out of bed and stretched vitality into his powerful, decaying body. That was fifty years ago, and he had been—let's see—twenty-four. He walked over to the window, a half-inch wall of plate glass that covered the cove side of the bedroom. On a good day he could see the white line of breakers at the bar, sometimes even the splinter-and-smudge of a coastal steamer. But this was not a good day.

A low mist lay over the town. The fog was thinning under the morning sun and through it, almost directly below, he saw the unpainted roofs of the houses in the Lower Hill development. Tala River separated the Lower Hill section from the business center. Mist steamed steadily from between the river banks and he could not see the brown water, but out through the fog poked the steel supports of Old Bridge

48

and the concrete arch of Cove Bridge. He looked down the smoky river to the mill—The Mill—the collection of machines and buildings that had put Cove on the map of the world. He could barely recall the thrill of the day he had bought it, a smoking wreck after the great fire of 1902; it had been a part of him too long for him to remember how he had felt before it was his. He stood by the window for a long time, staring at the mill sprawled along the shore like a giant's junkyard.

A bus, gray and streamlined, materialized out of the fog on the Cove highway and he followed it until it was out of sight behind the Cove Bank Building on Elm Street. He looked approvingly along Elm Street, with its two-story buildings, false-fronted and neon-lighted, built of lumber from the Cove Mill, repaired with plywood from the new plant, financed in whole or in part by men from the mill, tenanted by men who would not be what they were, nor where they were, if Old Herm's mill had not been slicing round stuff since 1902. Why, there weren't five big men in the community who had not worked for him at some time in their careers.

On the hogback between Elm Street and the north shore of the cove were scattered the huge, homely, pleasant houses of the Old-Timers, two or three a city block. They were three-storied, beamed with 8-by-12 spruce beams; they had stained-glass windows, and shutters; they had basements, for they were on ground that did not flood when a southwest wind and a high tide backed the river up onto Elm Street. These houses had been built by pioneers who became rich when Old Herm's mill put a town on the bottom land they had intended to farm. In one of these big houses, Peterson had lived until his wife died; then he moved into the Siwash Point house of his son-in-law.

Beyond the big houses on the hump, the land fell away to the beach, and the beach curved off toward the Pacific.

Far along the beach, just shadows in the mist, were the buildings of the new plywood plant that his son-in-law had built. But with my money, Peterson told himself as he turned from the window; if it wasn't for the old mill on the river, there wouldn't be any fancy new plywood plant up the cove. He sighed and pulled off the tight-fitting, tailor-cut red flannel pajamas that his daughter gave him every Christmas.

He took a cold shower, cheating a little with the warm water but making up for it by turning the force way up. He rubbed down vigorously, and as he dressed he felt fine. The doctors be damned: he felt wonderful, good as ever. He rolled his shoulders, feeling the muscles play across his broad back. By God, he was still good for a day's work.

Gordon was always talking about strikes, and there probably would be a strike. His daughter kept telling him, Gordon was smart. And her husband probably *was* smart: he had the mills making more money than ever, though that wasn't tough, with lumber selling for what it had since the war. But a man could be too smart, with his slide rules and public relations experts and Intelligence Departments. You can't buck a log with a slipstick, and you can't bust a strike with a press release.

The way to get men to work was to go out and lead them. Why, he remembered the time, back in '13 or '14, when the Wobblies were raising holy old hell. He hadn't gone fancy. He hadn't called in engineers with college degrees and the other high-priced hand-holders Gordon used. Instead, he'd called the men together and, standing on a stump, a peavey handle in one hand, he had stared them quiet, and then he had roared, "I'm Herm Peterson and I'm the best goddam man in these parts. Anybody who don't think so, just try to toss me off here."

Two of them had tried, one at a time, and failed.

Looking down on them, he had bellowed, "I can lick any bastard that can hear me."

No one else tried to climb the stump. They were silent.

"All right, men. I just wanted to show you I'm one of you. Now let's make lumber."

And taking an ax—he'd always liked an ax better than a cross-cut; he wasn't much good with a Swedish fiddle—he had gone out, taken his place on a springboard and felled a 200-foot Douglas fir, proud that he could still handle an ax so as to leave a splinterless, plane-smooth scarf.

After that there had been little trouble in Camp Five, and all along the line he'd had less trouble than any operator in the area. By God, he'd like to try it again. He could still handle the white-sheet punks that passed for loggers these days.

He finished dressing, put on the tweeds his daughter liked him to wear around the house, and went into the dining room. The paper was folded by his place at the table, but he did not open it. He was looking out the window again, this time north over the tops of the second-growth. As far as he could see—and much farther—stretched the land he had logged. In the Tala Valley above Cove the second growth was already forty years old and as thick as a man's body. He had logged up along the streams first, floating the round-stuff down to the mill. Then he had thrown tracks up the waterless valleys and brought out more; in time, he had laid more than three hundred miles of track. After the first hundred miles he'd stopped using the old joke, "My track isn't as long as the Northern Pacific, but it's just as wide," for he was too proud of his railroad to joke about it.

And now, though he had to reach across three counties for his lumber and the old mill had barely enough logs to keep one shift busy, the little portables he had devised—mills on wheels, mills that went to the timber—were at work miles back in the woods, cutting the patches that had been by-passed, making money out of stands other operators had argued were too costly to cut. Old Herm was still a good man at getting out lumber. He knew it. And he was glad others knew it.

He thought exclusively in terms of logging. Whenever he took a vacation, he thought of how he would log the timber he saw; and if there was no timber, he thought of how he would get it down to the saws if there were. Like the time Elizabeth had hauled him off to the Grand Canyon and she had thought it so funny when he said, "By God, it would take a real tyee logger to drive this river." That was the same trip when he had said of Pike's Peak, "You could get the stuff out of here with cats."

Elizabeth—lots of people—didn't like logged-off land. He couldn't see why. Stumpage meant problems solved; cut-over land was land that had been licked; it had yielded its lumber, people were living in and warming themselves by and flying and sailing on the yield of that land. A cut-over hill was money in the bank, a pay roll met, a new multiple gangsaw for the Mill or a new cat for the camps. And the hills that Old Herm logged were logged right. But Elizabeth had never understood.

He turned his attention to his grapefruit, and while he was eating it the cook came in with the bowl of oatmeal she prepared for him each morning.

"Where is Ruth, Agnes?"

"She is having breakfast in bed, sir."

He wished she would forget the sir stuff, at least when Ruth wasn't around. "And Gordon?"

"He ate early."

He sighed again. He did not like to eat alone. Conversation at mealtime did not matter to him—he had bolted too many meals in the ritual silence of the logging-camp mess to care about seasoning his food with words—but he liked the feel of someone else at the table. He unfolded the paper, propped it against the sugar bowl (Well, if Ruth was up he couldn't do that) and started on his oatmeal. He had read two short items halfway down the page before the heavy, sullen banner-line forced itself upon him:

LABOR LEADER'S WIFE SLAIN

Dee Dawson Killed
in Kitchen of Home

He read the headline over several times, and then read the first paragraph of the story.

He got up and went back to the great window in his bedroom and looked down at the houses in the Lower Hill district. The fog was thinner. He saw women moving in the back yards. He picked out the wooden spire of the Catholic Church, and counted off three blocks and two houses in the fourth block. That was Dawson's place, on the borderline between the Croatian and Finnish districts. It looked like all the others. It seemed to Peterson that the house should have some marks to show that inside was a man who had just lost his Elizabeth.

"The poor damn bastard," he thought. "The poor, goddam bastard."

Gordon Gentry's office was large and crowded: filing cabinets lined the walls; stacks of trade magazines were spotted on the floor; photostats of section maps were pinned on top of each other on all four walls. Black looseleaf notebooks leaned against each other on top of the filing cabinets, and three drawers full of papers balanced weirdly on a stool. The confusion centered around Gentry's desk, a huge, solid old walnut desk that was clear of papers except for two neat trays of letters, incoming and outgoing, and the morning edition of the *Logger*.

Gentry was reading the story of the murder. He had read it several times, and each time he liked it less.

His secretary came in. She was a tall, lean, dark-haired woman in her thirties, a widow from St. Paul; she was a good secretary, liked her work, and got along with her fellow workers. "He's here, Mr. Gentry."

"Barovich?"

"Yes, Mr. Gentry."

"Send him in. See that we're not disturbed."

"Yes, Mr. Gentry." She paused at the door and said, "He seems nervous."

"Send him in just the same."

Gentry lit a cigarette—his tenth of the morning, though he usually did not smoke that many in a day. He was breathing smoke when Barovich came in.

"Shut the door, Steve."

Barovich closed the door and pulled on the knob to make sure the latch had caught, which it had. He turned to face Gentry. Barovich was a little less than six feet tall. He weighed about a hundred seventy-five pounds and had the build of a good half-back; he had been a good half-back. His clothes were neat and conservative, and he wore them well. He was handsome. His hair was brown and straight and had recently been cut. He had brown eyes, a long straight nose, and high, Slavic cheekbones. His jaw was wide and his chin had a faint cleft. His mouth was large but the lips were firm, almost too thin. He was licking his lips as he stood facing Gentry, but his lips were not moist. Even after his tongue passed over them they were dry.

"Did you do it?"

"No."

"Then what makes you so nervous?"

"You know what makes me nervous."

"You said you didn't do it."

"I didn't."

"Then what makes you nervous?"

"I got there before he came home."

"It was done then?"

"Yes."

"Then he didn't do it?"

"Bull?"

"Yes, Bull."

"No."

"Sure?"

"He didn't, unless it was before he went to that meeting."

The men were silent. Each measured the other with his eyes as though expecting the familiar physique to have changed because their relationship had changed.

"If you did it," Gentry said, "you better tell me. I'll need to know. I may be able to fix things if I start now, but we can't let things slide."

"No. I didn't."

"Don't lie to me."

"I'm not lying." Barovich's voice rose, almost broke, and steadied on a higher pitch. He looked nervously at the door. "It wasn't me. And I don't think it was Bull."

"Who the hell else?"

"I don't know."

"Well, tell me what you do know."

Barovich swallowed a couple of times. He came over and sat down on the edge of the big desk, beside the outgoing file.

"I got there about nine. It was foggy as hell. The lights were on in the place, but I couldn't see anybody moving against them. I hung around outside a while, ten, fifteen minutes I think, without seeing anyone inside. So I went up on the porch and rang the bell, in case she was in bed or reading. Nobody came. I kept ringing about five minutes to make sure. So I went in."

"How?"

"I just tried the front door and it opened. I called, 'Is anybody in?' or something like that, but there wasn't any answer. I went over the living room. Nothing there. Half-dozen Book-of-the-Month books, nothing subversive. So I went in the bedroom. I was going through the dresser—there wasn't anything—when all of a sudden I got a feeling I ought to look in the kitchen. Jesus Christ, there she was, flat on her face."

"Did you look to see if she was dead?"

"Hell, no. She was dead all right. She sure as hell looked dead to me. I just got the hell out of there."

"Did you touch anything,"

"I had on gloves."

"How about footprints?"

"I may have left some, but I don't think so. I wiped my feet good when I went in."

"Did anyone see you hanging around?"

"In that fog?"

"It looks to me as if you're clear. What you worrying about?"

Barovich ran his finger along the edge of the desk. He watched Gentry out of the corner of his eye. "I think the cops know I've been doing this work."

Gentry took it without blinking, but when he lit another cigarette his hand was shaking. "How would they know?"

"They caught me busting in the Fish Packers' office last month."

"You son-of-a-bitch."

"Take it easy, Mr. Gentry. I suppose I should have told

you, but I wanted that money and I was afraid you might call me off. I didn't know this would happen."

"What did they do when they caught you?"

"Nothing."

"Nothing! For Christ sake! Nothing! Come on—spill it."

"I told the Chief what I was doing and he let me go."

"He just let you go?"

"Yes."

"And you told him who you were working for?"

"Yes. You and the League."

"You son-of-a-bitch."

"Well, he let me go."

"And you told him you were going to see what you could find out about Bull?"

"No."

"The hell you didn't."

"All right, I told him. He was all for it, too. Christ sake, Mr. Gentry, he don't like these labor bastards any better than you do. Why, he even fixed it for the prowl car not to be around Dawson's last night."

"That's wonderful. That's simply wonderful. So the Chief and half the cops know."

"No, just the Chief."

"Who arrested you?"

"Elliott."

"Did you tell him you were working for me?"

"No."

"Like hell."

"Like hell I did."

"What's he think about your getting off?"

"Probably that it was a fix. He's dumb, Elliott."

Gentry lit another cigarette from the stub of the one he'd been smoking. He leaned back in the swivel chair and grinned without pleasure. "She's a bitch, isn't she?"

"Yes."

"What if the chief can't find who did it and decides to pin it on you? He can sure as hell throw the hooks into you—you're a natural. And if Bull didn't do it, and you didn't do it, he may have a hell of a time finding who did it. And when the unions start yelling for blood, he'll have to find somebody. Got an alibi for last night?"

"My sister might cover for me."

"Where was she?"

"Home."

"She'd go down the line for you?"

"Yeah, I think so. Not for me—for mother."

"You may have to use her. But better try to think up something better. An alibi by a relative probably would sound phony. Anybody would figure she'd lie for you."

"Yeah. That's why I'm nervous."

"You ought to be nervous, you son-of-a-bitch. If you'd told me about getting arrested, you wouldn't be in this mess."

"You're in it, too."

"You're telling me."

"If I get nailed and you don't get me out, don't think I'll cover for you."

Gentry moved quickly, so quickly Barovich didn't have time to get his arm up before the slap reddened his cheek. "Don't threaten me. Any trouble I get in won't be half as hot as yours. Remember that."

"You got to help me."

"I'm helping you. But don't get the idea you can push me around."

Barovich stood up. "What are you going to do about it?"

"It would solve a lot of problems if Bull killed her."

"I don't think he did."

Gentry sucked in a lungful of smoke and expelled it. "I think he better have. It's the only answer." He stood up and put a hand on Barovich's shoulder. "Look, Steve, I'm sorry I lost my temper. You should have told me about getting caught, but you didn't, and it's water under the bridge. Now you be careful and I'll see what I can do for you. In the meantime, I'll keep paying you at the same rate." He opened his desk, took out an envelope and shook ten ten-dollar bills onto the desk. "A hundred a week."

Barovich picked up the money and crammed it into his pocket. "How you going to fix it?"

"Who said anything about fixing it? I'm sure Bull did it, and I intend to see him brought to justice."

"I get you."

"No hard feelings?"

"No hard feelings."

"I'll let you know tomorrow how things are going."

"Okay, Mr. Gentry."

"Tell Miss Walker to come in on your way out."

Barovich went out without looking back. Outside the office door he paused and his long, blunt-tipped fingers ran over his cheek.

He left the plywood plant without speaking to Miss Walker.

AFTERNOON

BILL ELLIOTT woke before the alarm. His wife was already up; he saw that she had folded his gray uniform, which he had dropped on the floor, neatly over the back of a chair. His broad belt was draped incongruously over the dresser mirror and the muzzle end of the holster was almost in an open jar of cold cream.

Propped on one elbow, Elliott rubbed a soft hand over his face. Gwenn came into the bedroom from the kitchen. She was a short, well-formed girl and was wearing a blue housecoat. "Going to sleep your life away?" she asked, employing a family joke.

He spanked at her backside and she twisted out of the way and smiled down at him. "Can't hit a moving target, hey, copper?"

"Come here, you."

She knelt on the bed and kissed him. Her breasts were heavy on his chest. His arms closed round her. And it was not until later that Bill Elliott thought about Dee Dawson.

Gale Seward got up a little after one that afternoon. He stood in his gray flannel pajamas and looked down at the paper spread out on the floor. He felt dull and drained. He did not like the paper: the make-up was weak and he should have got Dawson's name in the bannerline.

He dressed quickly and went out. At the corner drugstore he bought the *Oregonian*. Reading the headlines, he walked to the Goal Line Café for breakfast. The headlines cheered him: they were about some United Nations squabble; the *Oregonian* didn't have anything about the murder. He went into the Goal Line and slid onto a stool.

"Stack and ham?" the cook asked.

"Yeah, the usual."

"Coffee, cream only?"

"Coffee, black."

"One of those nights, eh?"

"One of those nights."

As he breakfasted, Seward listened to the conversations of the other customers. A few were talking about the murder. He could not hear much of what was being said, but their voices were dispassionate. The only men who were talking loud were some loggers disputing the distant merits of Ted Williams and Joe DiMaggio.

After a second coffee, he walked to the office. Most days he avoided the office until evening, when the ad chasers and the bookkeeping girls had cleared out. While the commercial side was in possession, he felt out of place in the front office. The business end of the paper was alien to him. At night the *Logger* had a different personality, combined of many elements—Joe Kalinen, a rumpled cherub beerily batting out messy copy about county-seat shenanigans or the beauty of the season's first night-blooming cereus; young Frank Velecich fretting out new alliterations to apply to the sundry sports celebrities whose activities concerned him; Helene Lewis, her daily chronicle of the lumbertown society complete, reading the early galleys of proof. All this was the *Logger* he identified himself with. In daylight the paper was something else.

He went in. Helene Lewis was at her Underwood, typing with two fingers of each hand. The boss sat at Seward's desk; he was reading the advance proofs for the next month's features.

The boss—Rutherford B. Olson—was a short, fat, deeply tanned man with an aura of thin, silvery hair and a sparse gray goatee that looked like an oversight. He had served three terms as United States Senator and still dwelt on the experience. Seeing Seward, he boomed heavily, "A fine story, my boy, a fine story. You do honor to your profession. Reporting like that makes me want to get back in the saddle."

Seward was past amazement, or even amusement, at the Boss's metaphors. And since it was not yet time for another of the Boss's biennial seizures of repertorial fervor, he was not worried that the old man would try to do some work on the Dawson story. So he said, "Thanks."

"Do you anticipate a solution? Do you feel you can solve this mystery?"

"No," Seward said sharply. And then to cover his annoyance, "I got an agreement with the chief. He solves the murders and I write the stories."

"Delighted," rumbled the Boss, "simply delighted." Teddy Roosevelt had been one of Olson's early heroes and he always emphasized the first syllable of the word delighted. "I want to see superb reporting, my boy, a recrudescence of the distinguished journalism which marked the *Logger* in the olden days and made it the biggest little morning paper on the Coast."

Seward said, "Sure."

The Boss made him nervous. He was always afraid that one of Olson's remarks would touch off his own temper, and he did not want to lose his job: he liked running the paper. The type of journalism which had marked the *Logger* in the olden days, he thought bitterly, was not distinguished, although it was certainly distinctive. After the voters had put the Boss out in 1930, Olson resumed active management of the *Logger* for the first time in twenty years. He had the courage of his prejudices. He attacked government relief at a time when the Mill was down and two-thirds of the workers were unemployed. He tried to convince his readers that anyone who took money from the government was a collectivist bum. He suggested that Judge Lynch had the answer for labor agitators in general and Harry Bridges in particular. In 1936 the town went Democratic, four to one; and a few months later, when the Supreme Court killed NRA, Olson ran a six-column spread of the Blue Eagle and, over it, in Second Coming type, the caption:

The Vulture is Dead

At this point the paid circulation of the *Logger* was below the five hundred mark. The circulation manager was receiving letters that threatened the newsboys with birdshot or rock salt if they continued to deliver the sheet over the protests of householders who resented having Olson's opinions thrown on their front porches.

Then the bank stepped in. The bank officials were tactful. They called Olson "Senator" and complimented his courage and agreed with his opinions. But they also made sure he hired a managing editor to make the *Logger* more of a newspaper. Olson never seemed to realize that he had lost control of his paper. He did not resent Gale Seward, especially since Seward devoted himself to news and the Boss thought a paper was its editorial page. All his animosity was directed toward the Democrat "who used the Depression to steal my office," and against the Republican state committeemen who euchered him out of renomination and re-election in 1942.

Even after long association, Seward was not sure whether the Boss clung to his prejudices because he was one of the bravest men in the world, or because he was one of the stupidest. He was not sure whether he should admire or dislike Olson.

Now he went into the backshop and climbed the ladder to the platform where the files of old papers were kept. There, alone, standing before the accumulated history of the town, he was no longer able to keep from thinking of the night before. He recalled what Elliott had said, what he himself had promised. And it seemed to Seward that he had let himself be carried away. He had no more right to take part in a campaign to break the Chief, than the Boss had to put his political opinions in headlines or leave out news that displeased him. His job was to report news, not make it.

But if Steve Barovich had killed Dee Dawson, that was news.

He went back through the files until he came to the story of the Thanksgiving Day game that Barovich had lost. The game was against Sawtown, Cove's nearest neighbor and bitterest rival. Cove was leading, 13 to 12, in the closing minutes of the game. Barovich intercepted a pass and, groggy after making a hard tackle on the previous play, ran the wrong way. Thirty yards. One of his teammates tackled him on the five-yard line. On the next play, Barovich dropped back to punt; a low pass from center slithered away from him; he fell on it behind the goal line, scoring a safety—two points —for the Sawyers. The final score was 14 to 13, Cove losing.

Seward clapped the pages of the file together and slid it back in the case and went back to the front office. The Boss had gone, but Helene Lewis was still working on her society copy. He sat on the edge of her desk. "Hello, prim and proper, how's my favorite female reporter?"

"Lousy," she replied, without raising her eyes from the keyboard. She finished her story, rolled out the paper and looked up at him. She had green eyes, remarkably large and clear, quite beautiful. She also had beautiful legs, but they were out of sight under the desk. Otherwise she was rather plain; round-shouldered, small-breasted. She wore her brown hair in braids and she dressed in plain brown dresses that were almost a uniform. "I'm feeling low."

"Was she a friend of yours?"

"Who? Oh, you mean Dee. No."

"What ails thee then, my long-tressed lass?"

"For one thing, I've got the curse."

"Oh."

She traced the part in her hair with an unshined fingernail, patted the coiled braids at the back of her neck, and said, "Which one of us do you think it is? I think it's Ted and he thinks it's me. I always feel as if I'd done all I need to."

"You embarrass me," Seward said, truthfully. "No, you both look virile enough. Or Ted looks virile and you look capable, to be precise."

"Thank you, kind sir. But if he doesn't make me pregnant next month I'm going to Portland and see about this artificial insemination business."

"Pardon a blushing bachelor for shifting the conversation from such an interesting subject; but what do you know about Steve Barovich?"

"He lost the Thanksgiving Day game."

"That was ten years ago. He must have done something since then."

"I think he works at the plywood plant. Lives at home with his mother. She's a nice old lady, doesn't speak much English—they're Crows, of course—and his sister. His father's dead. Died since you came to town, I think. That's about all I know. He doesn't get around a lot—to parties and things."

"What sort of a guy is he?"

"Sort of nice-looking. One of those big, tall Crow kids who can pass for an Indian any place there aren't Indians. Real quiet, too. I don't know him very well, but he's always impressed me as being real quiet. A well-mannered kid. Polite, I mean."

"He ever been in any trouble you can remember?"

"A few years ago there was talk about him and some married gal. But she was Croatian too, and you know how the Crows keep something like that to themselves. They were all Catholics, so there wasn't any divorce action or anything. Do you think Steve had something to do with Dee Dawson?"

"Don't go jumping to conclusions, prim and proper. For the record, I've got a hunch he's been putting sponges up the coin slots of pay telephones." He got off the desk and stretched. "Joe been in?"

"At this hour?"

"I can dream, can't I? If he comes in, tell him to flag his fanny down to the coroner's office and get the dope about when the inquest will be held. We didn't get anything at all from the coroner last night."

"All right. The great reporter is to see the coroner about the inquest. I'll tell him. And I'll bet you five dollars he comes in stewed, with his hat on the back of his head and his sound-track straight from Hollywood. A real live murder is going to bring out the Winchell in him."

"No bet."

Seward picked up the little green phone book, opened to the B's, and looked up Barovich. Three Baroviches—Anton, F. L., and Katya. He wrote down Katya's address. "I'll probably be in early," he told Helene from the door.

"Don't strain yourself," she said as she clipped a recipe from the *Oregonian*. "I read a book in school once. It said, 'Murder will out.'"

Seward walked rapidly across town. The fog had lifted and it was a fine afternoon. A gentle wind blew down the cove from the ocean and carried with it the triumphant whistle of a purse seiner announcing a safe crossing of the bar. The air was cool and sharp with salt. He paused on the Old Bridge and watched the brown water, opaque as molasses and not much faster, ooze by. He found a rusty nail and with his toe nudged it over the edge of the walk; the nail vanished in the brown flow and a tiny circle of ripples moved on with the current and were gone. He looked for another nail but didn't find one, and walked on.

Katya Barovich's house lay eight blocks north of Dawson's, at the outskirts of the Lower Hill development; it had been built earlier than most of the places on that side of the river. The house had two stories and nine rooms—but no basement —the distinction that separated it most obviously from the homes of the Old Settlers. The lawn was fine, though, and the shrubs that old Felix Barovich—Steve's father—had planted in a brief period of prosperity were now large enough to shut light from the first-floor windows.

Gale Seward was standing on the porch before he fully realized that he had no real excuse for asking Steve for an interview. It would scarcely do to say, "Did you kill Dee Dawson last night?" And the only other question he could think of was, "Does it still bother you, running the wrong way with that pass?" That would hardly do, either. And, by his appearance, he was warning Barovich. He hesitated. The hell with it. He'd just play it straight and tell Barovich that he'd heard Barovich had some information about Dawson: that ought to get an interesting reaction.

He rang the bell a second time and heard inside the slow, hollow beat of steps on a thin carpet. The door was opened by a young woman.

"I'd like to speak to Steve Ba—" he began, and halted in mid-sentence. The girl who had opened the door, a tall girl wearing a heavily embroidered peasant blouse and a wool skirt, was the girl he had surprised the night before in Dawson's kitchen.

"Steve isn't here," she said, and shut the door in his face. He rang the bell several times, but she did not answer.

Seward walked back to a grocery a few blocks toward the center of town and phoned the Barovich house. A girl's voice said "Hello," but when he said, "This is Gale Seward, may—" she hung up. The next time there was no answer.

He gave up. He felt like a drink. He walked back to town and went to the Elks Club. The bar was almost deserted. The barkeep, a husky, deeply tanned Finn whose skin was darker than his hair, leaned over a portable chess board, replaying from a book the 1911 game between Lasker and Thomas. A resident of the club read the ads in a *Saturday Evening Post*. Another was drinking a beer as though he did not like beer. Seward got a whiskey and soda and took it to a booth in a corner, away from the windows, and nursed it along while he tried to decide what he should do about the Barovich girl. He was on his second whiskey, and still undecided, when Chief Snow came in, changed a five-dollar bill at the bar, and went over to the slot machines. From the shadowed ambush of his booth, Seward watched Snow, who stood spraddle-legged before the two-bit machine, his left hand feeding in quarters, his right working the lever.

The fruit-spangled wheels spun and halted within their ordained limits of chance. Snow was lucky. Three times the combinations of cherries and lemons came up to send quarters clanking down the chute, and once he lined up three plums; sustained by these refunds, he played nearly a quarter of an hour before running out of money. A half-dozen men drifted over to watch him play; they rooted for him against the machine; they cheered him on with grunts and groans and cries of *ooh,* and *damn,* and *That was ka-lose.*

Snow went to the bar and gave the Finn another five-dollar bill.

"Dimes?" the barkeep asked, his thoughts still centered on the chess game of 1911.

"Quarters," Snow said sharply. He always played the quarter machine. He liked to stand in this mahogany-and-leather room, surrounded by competent, dollar-making men and dollar-costing drinks, and bet against odds he knew he could not beat. He liked to have an audience kid him as he fed money into the machine.

He put a lot of money into the machines. One night, after he had spent more than a hundred dollars to make the fruited wheels revolve, Mayor Everett had asked, "Think you ought to spend so much on those things, Rajah?"

And Snow, a little drunk, had leaned on his shoulder and whispered, "Politics. The boys in the club like to think of the Chief of Police as a sucker. If I didn't play, just cause I know the odds on these things, they'd think I was stuck up. Bad politics. This way, I'm one of them."

A little drunk when he made this speech, he believed it himself, as did the mayor, who was more than a little drunk. But it was not the real reason he liked to play the quarter machine: he enjoyed it because he could not afford the losses; and the reason he liked to lose more than he could afford lay deep in his past, so deep he could only remember the kind of details you use in filling out forms.

His father had been killed in a mill accident up on Grays Harbor, and a year later his mother was sent to the state mental hospital; Roger went down to Cove to live with his aunt—a gaunt, tubercular woman whose existence was a prolonged complaint against the climate that was killing her, and his uncle—the poverty-plagued minister of a small and ridiculed church. He had been lonely: he was not allowed to play with the sons of fishermen and millworkers and foreigners, and he had received few invitations to visit the big houses of the Old-Timers on the hogback.

And then there had been the sudden miracle of acceptance. He'd been working on the docks, breaking strike—though he thought of it simply as work, when the striking longshore-

men broke through the line of police. Snow was rolling barrels aboard a tanker and was coming down the gang with an
empty dolly when the longshoremen started up. He fought
them off for a minute or two, how long he never knew—for
there is no way of judging time at moments like that—and
then he went down, unconscious, without knowing what hit
him. When he came to, in the hospital, his broken head
wrapped in bandages, the nurse read to him from the *Logger*
a story in which he was compared to Horatius at the bridge,
and was called a defender of the sacred rights of the American
working man. After that he belonged, almost, to the group
that his aunt, who had died the year before, had called The
Better Element. He was asked to join clubs—all except the
Masons—and he did join; he met some of the businessmen,
and some of the politicians, and when Everett became mayor,
Snow had been his surprise selection as Chief of Police. That
was fourteen years ago, and though Everett had been out of
office twice, the interim mayors had not tried to appoint
anyone else. Snow was a popular Chief, except with the agitators. He belonged.

Snow fed the second five dollars into the machine, getting
back only six quarters, which he played back. "Tough luck,
Chief," said one of the audience when the last quarter was
gone.

"Lucky in love," said another. Snow looked at him sharply,
for the Chief's matrimonial difficulties were not an unshared
secret, but the fellow was just making conversation. He smiled
at Snow and said, "Bad business, that last night."

"Very bad."

"Bull killed her, didn't he, Chief?"

"I couldn't say." He walked toward the bar, and two of the
men went with him. They knew Snow well as a man; they
could anticipate what he would do in any situation around
the club: but as Chief, he was something different. They did

not know what it was to be a police chief. How would one go about being chief of police? His brisk, "I couldn't say," hinted a mysterious efficiency, and they thought of Scotland Yard officials in the movies, brilliant and implacable behind great desks in dusty rooms.

"But if Bull did it, you'll get him, won't you?" the first man said.

Snow thought the question over for a moment. His men had found nothing to implicate Bull. Nor had Steve Barovich come in, as Snow had expected, to report on what had gone wrong during his visit to the Dawson house. "If Bull did it, we'll get him," he said at last.

"You're damn tooting," agreed the second man. "We were talking it over at lunch today and we said that this time Bull had gone too far. Maybe you can strike and call God-fearing Americans fascists, maybe, but you can't kill your wife, not in America, and get away with it. This isn't Moscow."

"I'm glad to hear you're after him, Rajah," the first Elk put in. "It's time somebody had guts enough to get that guy."

They reached the bar, where Lasker had just repeated his 1911 victory over Sir Charles.

"Don't you ever get tired of that stuff?" Snow asked the Finn. The barkeep looked up from his study of the checkmate. "No."

"What's there in it?"

"Only game I know where luck doesn't play a part. Any trouble you get in is your own fault. It's not a question of fate or—"

"Three Scotches," interrupted Snow.

And the first Elk said, "Now as I was saying, Rajah, you can see what it will mean to the community to have this cleared up right away. It will look like hell if it seems a man can get away with killing his wife, just because he's a labor leader."

Snow wished he could get away from this; he didn't want to be put in the position of promising he'd arrest Bull. He looked around the room and saw Gale Seward watching him from the corner booth. "Pardon me, fellows," he said, picking up his drink, "I have to see Scoop over here about a story. See you later."

Seward was surprised to see the Chief coming toward him. But he welcomed the visit—it saved him a trip to the station. He greeted Snow with, "How goes it, Chief?"

Snow shook his head. "I'm going to have to give the boys an injection of bloodhound blood. They haven't picked up a thing."

"How's Bull stand?"

"Clear, as far as I can tell."

"Think you're going to have to call roll on the ones who rolled her?"

Snow looked blank, then remembered his conversation with Seward the night before. "Could be," he said.

Seward swirled the ice around the bottom of his glass. "I was wondering. Do you think a woman could have done it?"

"It's possible. That steam iron was pretty heavy for a woman to swing, but of course women use them all the time. That's an angle, all right." He aimed his chin at Seward. "Got a candidate?"

"No, I just thought it might have been the girl friend of somebody she was playing around with." He remembered what Mac had said the night before about his lack of a poker face, and to change the subject he told Snow about his conversation with Nellie the night before.

At that moment, Nellie was lying back in the big chair in her room, an old *Reader's Digest* in her lap.

She pecked away at a story about a paralyzed girl who was the best telephone saleswoman in New Orleans. She ordinarily liked everything in the *Digest,* but this story vaguely irritated her. She gave up and flipped through the magazine, reading the jokes. They did not amuse her. She closed the magazine and looked out the window, across the tarpaper wasteland of two roofs, into the window of an apartment where a fat blonde was cooking something on an electric range. The blonde turned and saw Nellie looking; she stared back briefly across the little distance that separated them, and pulled down the cracked and yellow blind.

It had happened before.

Nellie got wearily out of her chair and went to the kitchen. Mrs. Dothan, the madam, and Irish, the other girl, were at the kitchen table, which was covered with oilcloth and littered with dirty plates from the breakfast they had just finished. They said good morning.

"It's afternoon. And what's good about it?"

"The fog lifted," said Mrs. Dothan.

"So what?"

"Aren't you feeling well, Nell?" Mrs. Dothan's solicitude was genuine, and annoying.

"I'm all right."

Nellie looked in the icebox but saw nothing inspiring: beer and cold cuts and two bottles of milk, beheaded of cream. She poured herself a cup of coffee from the Silex and sat down. "Jeez, I'll bet I didn't get three hours sleep all night."

Mrs. Dothan said, "Maybe you better see a doctor, dear."

"I got to see Jonesey tomorrow."

"I mean a real doctor."

"I'm all right."

Irish, a dark, tight-featured girl in her early twenties, glanced up from the crossword puzzle she was working. "Maybe it's the change of life."

"Maybe." Nellie didn't feel up to a fight. "Anything in the paper?"

"Naw," Irish said, disappointed in her failure. "Some local babe got herself murdered."

"They catch the guy who did it?"

"No," said Mrs. Dothan, taking over Irish's share of the conversation. "And I think it's a real shame that the police don't give better protection." She patted her gray hair into place and added, "I mean, what's the use of paying taxes and having a police force if they let murderers run around loose? It makes me uneasy when I think of all the men who call here."

"They don't come here to kill anybody," said Nellie.

"I mean it's just that I think that kind of people ought to be locked up."

Irish swore softly. "These crosswords! They're too damn tough. Look at this. Eighty-two vertical, 'Athenian courtesan, fourth century B.C.,' in six letters, for Christ sake."

Bull Dawson woke from a hard, snoring, drugged sleep. The sun was in his face. He awoke alone in the double bed and he lay staring at the island spots that overflowing gutters had stained on the ceiling. And then, suddenly and fully, he remembered.

He remembered the shock and disgust, the wave of panic, the growing hopelessness. He remembered the open mouth, the bloody clot of hair on the iron, the half-pressed suit, the smell of burned-out coffee pot on the range.

Rolling stiffly out of bed, he shook his head but could not shake off the ache. Automatically he pulled on his pants and walked barefooted into the bathroom; he relieved himself, washed, brushed his teeth, examined his beard in the mirror, decided against a shave, and walked through the empty bedroom to the kitchen. The ironing board stood in the middle of the floor and he picked it up, folded its legs in, and opened the closet door.

Not till then did the tears come. He stood in the kitchen, his forehead against the closet door, and he wept.

— V —

EVENING

LOOKING out of the small window that faced the ocean, the old man saw a gull kiting against the wind on steady wings. He watched the gull until it rode an air current up and out of sight. Then he rolled face down on the dirty bed and tried not to think.

He felt sick.

He scooped in breath in shallow little mouthfuls, trying to keep his chest from moving and his head from aching. It didn't work. He gulped in a great lungful of air and pain exploded back of his eyes. And when it went away, the thought started to come back—the thought he would not, could not, must not think.

He got up and staggered to the door of the cabin and put his finger down his throat. There was nothing left to come up, but as his body was racked with nausea, the thought he must not think, the memory he must not recall, faded away.

He went weakly back to the cot and lay down.

Logger Hall was a two-story clapboard building on the bank of the Tala River. In the early days, its lower floor housed the Red Dog Saloon, its upper floor had cribs, and there were the inevitable rumors about a trap door through which bodies plunged into the river. The building was still painted barn red.

Because of its rowdy reputation, some of the union officials had objected to buying the hall for their local headquarters. But Bull had argued, "What the hell, our boys are used to coming here."

75

And the price was low.

In front of the barnlike building, standing in the light that fell from a lone bulb high on a telephone pole, Bull Dawson looked like a lost child. His nickname stemmed not from his physique but from a character named Dawson who had been in a comic strip popular during his high school days: he was a slender man, and this night, dressed in a tight-fitting leather jacket and neatly pressed, neatly darned black pants, he looked slight. Since waking that afternoon, Dawson had done many difficult things, but now, waiting outside the hall, he braced himself for one of his toughest jobs—facing the massed sympathy of his friends. He saw someone coming down the street and knew he could stall no longer. He went up the steps, and in.

Five loggers were lounging in the main hall, a big, bare room with a splintered ping-pong table, a new pool table, a few easy chairs and some benches stacked against the walls. When they saw Dawson the men stood up. Each hoped the other would think of the right thing to say, and nobody said anything; they stood uneasily with *Police Gazettes* and *Ranch Romances* still in their hands.

"Yeah, I know, fellas. Thanks."

"When's the funeral, Bull?"

"Day after tomorrow. They got to have the inquest first."

"We'll be there."

"Thanks, fellas. Anybody upstairs?"

"Leo came in a while back."

"I better see him."

The loggers did not sit down until he was out of sight up the stairs.

A narrow corridor bisected the second floor. Offices—they had been cribs—opened off each side. At the end of the corridor was a large room, where, in the heyday of the Red Dog, the girls had on Saturday night staged circuses for loggers who demanded more than standard entertainment.

Leo Plotch, Jack Winter and Arne Toivenen were in the office. Plotch was a tall, spectacularly thin man with a beaked nose and lead-gray hair, which he wore in a pompadour. Plotch was one of the first white men born in Cove County; an emotional speaker, he delighted in thundering at hecklers, "Is it un-American to be born in this country?" When still a young man, he had owned a mill. The great fire of 1902 wiped him out; forced to work for other operators, he grew bitter. He joined the I.W.W. in the early days and was active until the Wobblies split among themselves. Then he dropped out, refusing to take part in the internal disputes. "I only hate bosses," he would say; "the hell with fighting other workers." He was the union's business agent.

Winter, the treasurer, was a hard-boiled German with an eye-to-eye scar on his forehead to testify to his first-hand experience in a high-balling logging camp. He was a good treasurer, from the standpoint of other treasurers; his books were neat and clear, and at meetings he raised the point of policy costs. Plotch sometimes complained good-naturedly, but meaning it, "Holy o' Christ, boy, you act like the main thing a union should do is put money in the bank."

Toivenen, the secretary, was in his early thirties. He had been born after his father, an immigrant Finn, was killed in a strike riot at Astoria. He had an enormous, bony, fleshless face, tremendous courage, and almost no sense of humor. He was a devout, orthodox Communist.

They stopped talking when Dawson came in, and Toivenen took his feet off the desk. Plotch said, "I'm sorry as hell, Bull."

"Thanks." Dawson unzipped his leather jacket and hung it on the doorknob. Winter offered him his chair and he took it, then realized Winter didn't have a seat and said, "Oh, hell,

Jack, pardon me all to hell. I didn't . . ." His voice trailed off. Winter sat on the edge of the desk. Toivenen went to the square safe that crouched in a corner and took out a bottle of cheap whiskey. He handed it to Dawson. Dawson took a long drink and shuddered. He took a second drink, shorter, and capped the bottle. "I needed that. What's new?"

Plotch said, "Nothing with us." And after a pause, "Do you want to talk about it?"

"No."

Toivenen said, "Maybe you better, though."

"All right." He leaned back in the chair and stared unseeingly at the frameless engraving of Roosevelt pinned on the wall. "I can talk about it." There was a silence that seemed long to each man, though it lasted only seconds.

"What do you want to know?" Bull said.

Toivenen said, "How close to accurate was the story in the paper this morning?"

"I haven't read the paper." He was silent a moment. "I guess I'm the only guy in town who hasn't read the paper." He blinked rapidly, then shut his eyes.

"Jesus, Bull, I hate to ask you. But we got to know. Can you tell us about last night?"

"Yeah," Dawson opened his eyes. "Give me that bottle."

"Take it easy on the dehorn stuff," Winter warned. "It's straight tiger piss."

"Sure." Dawson took two gulps. He held the uncapped bottle in his hand as he talked, and when he felt he might cry, he took a drink. He told them about leaving the Hall and walking home through fog thick enough to carve your initials on. He'd stopped at the Goal Line for a hamburg and coffee, but remembered, before the hamburg was ready, that he'd promised to take her out to the Slipper after the meeting, and so he gulped the coffee and took the hamburger with him. He'd even picked out the onions.

He told them about finding Dee.

As Dawson talked, Plotch looked at him. Toivenen studied him, the Finn's blue eyes seldom blinking. Winter sat with his hand over his eyes, thumb and forefinger touching the ends of the scar on his forehead.

Toivenen asked, "Was your house gone over?"

"I didn't notice anything last night. I looked around again today. The place is sort of mussed up, but I guess the cops did that. There's nothing missing. There was some money in the dresser and it's still there. Dee had on the watch I gave her and her wedding and engagement rings. Her purse was in the bedroom. About twelve bucks in it."

"What about your papers? Things like that."

He shook his head.

Toivenen pressed on. "Any subversive books?"

"Some novels. She subscribed to a book club for a while. And some magazines—*Collier's* the *Digest,* crap like that. I'm not a party member. You ought to know that."

"I know. But they don't. Any letters?"

"Just personal stuff. Far as I can tell, it wasn't touched."

Plotch said, "How were the cops?"

"All right."

Toivenen said, "No rough stuff?"

"No. They asked a hell of a lot of questions, over and over. But they were okay. The Chief gave me some pills so I could get some sleep."

Plotch said, "They were around today checking on your alibi. You think they were in on it?"

"Huh?"

"You think it could have been the cops?"

"Jesus Christ, Leo, I don't know what to think. I can't think. Not yet. Don't you see? I just came home and found her dead, that's all." He took another drink. The liquor did not give him any lift.

Winter took his hand from over his eyes. "What comes next?"

"Inquest's tomorrow. They can't have the funeral until the day after that. The funeral will be the next day. Day after tomorrow."

Toivenen asked, "What about the inquest?"

"It's tomorrow."

"I know. But what are you going to do?"

"I got to be there. They said I should."

"Sure you got to be there. That's not what I mean. What are you going to say? Are you going to ram it to them? Ram it in and break it off?"

Dawson didn't say anything. He sat looking at the bottle; he wished he could get drunk; he had a feeling that if he could get drunk and lie down and sleep it off, when he woke up Dee would be frying eggs. But he couldn't get drunk. He took another drink, but afterward Toivenen was still talking. The words went on and on.

"They must have done it, Bull. Who else could have done it? It must of been them. She's a martyr, Bull, a martyr to the working class, and you owe it to her to get up on your hind legs tomorrow at that inquest and sound off. Name names. Give the League hell. Accuse them of hiring finks to break and enter. Pour it to them."

"But I don't know who did it."

"They must of."

"It could have been a burglar. It might have been anybody. I can't just accuse them of this. I got to know. I got to know first." He brushed his hair back off his forehead. "You don't seem to realize. Dee's dead. She won't come back. I can't just . . ." His voice trailed off. He cupped his forehead in his hands and rested his elbows on his knees.

"They killed my father," Toivenen said. His voice was low and harsh. "They shot him dead. He had a wooden pole

in his hand and they had Springfields, and they shot him dead.
Mother told me about it. And now they've killed your wife.
I'm thirty-four. Thirty-four years, and they're still killing.
And if you don't get up off your ass and ram it to them tomorrow, they'll be killing thirty years from now. Tomorrow's
your chance. They can't sue you for what you say tomorrow.
You may never get another chance like this. For Christ sake,
they control the court and the press. The only time you'll
ever be able to talk is tomorrow. You've got the public with
you now. They got to be with you. It's a hell of a thing to
have to capitalize on, Bull, but you can damn well bet they're
planning right now to turn this to their advantage. You're
just letting them make a sucker out of you if you don't use
that inquest for a sounding board. You've got to demand
justice. You've got a duty to Dee."

Plotch said, "Leave him alone. He's all gooned out."

"But you got to, Bull. Don't you see? You got to."

Dawson got to his feet. He looked small standing next to
Plotch. He stared a long time at each of the three men,
leaning slightly toward the man he was looking at. Suddenly
he ran out of the room. He forgot his leather jacket.

The men looked at each other.

"Holy o' Christ, man," Plotch said to Toivenen, "sometimes I think you got no heart in you at all."

Toivenen was breathing hard, and he had to swallow his
Adam's apple before speaking. "It wrings me out just looking
at him. I was damn near bawling, Leo. But there are things
you got to do. He's got to snap out of it."

Winter said, "I wish he wasn't drinking. It looks like hell,
a union president getting plastered."

Plotch said, "He needs it."

"I know. But it looks like hell."

Outside, Bull Dawson leaned against the telephone pole,
the pale light falling on his brown hair. He wished there were

some place to go besides the house. But he couldn't think of any.

He walked alone down the street, going slowly, and when he came to the bridge he stopped and looked at the water, black under the black sky, a moving blackness. There was a moon, but it gave no light; a cold moon. The water would be cold, too. He shook off a shudder and, alone, started on across the bridge.

Ahead, high above him, lights shone in the great window of the Gentry house. He wondered without bitterness whether they were having a party.

The linen was soft, smooth, silvery. The flames of the candles rose straight and high, unflickering. Beyond the glass wall, the town lay soft in the night; the lights in the windows below were muted. Beyond the town, the thin moon beat a streak of light onto the pewter bowl of the cove. And beyond the cove, beyond the white, frothy menace of the breaker line, the sea curved to the horizon.

At the table Herm Peterson talked of the old days, the good old days when loggers loved to let a little sun into the woods. A man was proud to have seen such days, by God, when loggers knew they were the toughest and the best, and were satisfied with their knowledge.

The others listened only for the pauses, and then they tried to interrupt. They were all men whom Peterson had made; but he had made them long ago and now the power to create success had passed to his son-in-law and they no longer had to listen closely or grunt appreciatively when he paused.

Ruth Gentry was uncomfortable as her father ran through his repertoire of reminiscences. She kept looking at his expensive suit that had the effect of lengthening his broad body, even of thinning his bull neck. She remembered when he had substituted fine cigars for the snoose he once used. But with all the changes, he was still the logger who had wept when she was born a girl, and he was still the old roughneck who had stood out so among the parents who came to visit her schoolmates at seminary and college.

"I'm sure we all know the story about the Dutchmen and the sauerkraut, Dad," she interrupted. Her voice was thin, and she was thin. She had beautiful red hair and that parboiled pink skin and pale, red-rimmed eyes that so often accompany it.

"Maybe Bob doesn't," said Old Herm, looking at Robert Kizer, the president of the bank. "He's a Dutchman and he ought to hear about it. Seems these Dutchmen, you know, the Bueller boys, had a stump ranch way up the Tala, and all they could grow was cabbage—"

"I believe you told me that one," Kizer said.

"All they could grow was cabbage," Old Herm rumbled, ignoring the interruption and Ruth's frantic look. "And they grew a hell of a lot—pardon me, Ruth—a whale of a lot of cabbage, but then they couldn't haul it to market. They couldn't carry it on horseback and there wasn't a wagon road. So they made sauerkraut out of it, put it in barrels and tried to drive it down the Tala, like round-stuff. It went all right at first, but there was a barrel jam at Folding Chair Rapids, you know, where there's that double turn, and they had to blast to break it up. All the staves gave way. And for five years after that you couldn't catch a trout on the Tala unless you baited with wieners, so they could have wieners with their sauerkraut."

Al Englund, the secretary of the Chamber of Commerce, leaned back from lighting a cigar on one of the candles. "Couple of stumpers up the valley growing pretty good cabbage now," he remarked.

Peterson fumbled in his vest pocket for a cigar. "That so? Did I ever tell you about the trouble we had with—"

Ruth broke in desperately, "Oh, I've been meaning to ask. Can any of you well-informed citizens tell me who murdered Delight Dawson?"

In the silence that followed she could hear the faint hiss of the burning candles and the rustle of starched linen as the men breathed. To the men at the table, Delight Dawson had been a person: a beautiful woman they had all seen and thought about. But to Ruth, Delight Dawson was remote and impersonal.

By standing, Ruth could have seen the moss-streaked roof of the house where she was born. Even nearer was the gray wooden school she had attended until her mother died. The people whose shadows moved across the lighted windows in the town below were the boys and girls she had grown up with, or their parents, or their children. But between Ruth and her early past had been driven a wedge—the bitter memory of her wedding day.

Her wedding in 1932 had been the most elaborate in the history of Cove. Old Herm had told her to spend as much as she wanted. Private cars were chartered to transport wedding guests from Seattle and San Francisco. A wing of the hotel was leased for a week; an interior decorator flew north from Los Angeles to redesign the banquet hall for the reception. The caterers came from California; the wine from France. When the state liquor store failed to have enough Scotch, a special shipment was ordered from New York. The day before the wedding, flowers were flown in from as far east as Montana, as far south as Sacramento. When Gordon had suggested that with the Mill down and the camps closed, such lavishness might be resented, Ruth thought he was merely disguising a male dislike for social display. "Nonsense, darling," she told him, "it puts money in circulation. Everybody will love it." And it *had* been a beautiful wedding, up to the point where that awful little man threw the stink bomb. After that, things had been difficult. There was the ordeal of leaving the church, with the sullen, dirty crowd standing silent in the street. . . . And the rock that had cracked the windshield.

After her marriage, Ruth Peterson Gentry took little part in the social life of Cove, other than to entertain her husband's business associates. She did no charity work.

And now, as the men stared down the table at her after her question about Dee Dawson, she smiled and said gaily, "Don't look so thunderstruck, gentlemen, or I'll think you really do know."

"Dawson killed her," the Chamber of Commerce secretary said.

"What makes you think so, Al?" Peterson asked.

"He'd do anything, that guy."

"No," said Peterson, glad of a chance to contradict them, "not that. I don't think he'd kill his wife. That's a hell of a thing to say about a man."

Wilfred Haines, the youngest man at the table, a thirty-five-year-old real estate promoter who was president of the Promote Prosperity League, said, "Well, I'll be damned. I never thought I'd live to see you sticking up for that Red, Mr. Peterson."

Peterson turned abruptly to his son-in-law, who sat silent and intent at the head of the table. "Did we send flowers?"

"No, but we will." Gentry pushed back his chair. "And now if you'll excuse us, Dad, Ruth, I've got something to talk over with the boys."

"Business?" asked Peterson, his deep voice edged with petulance.

"The Jamboree," said Gentry.

"Why don't you make it a real old-time affair with birling

and street dancing and— Did I ever tell you about the time we let the whor—fancy ladies have a booth at the carnival and—"

"That's an idea. We'll consider it, Dad," Gentry said, getting up. He ushered his three visitors into the den. It was a small room, rich with mahogany and leather, and it looked older than the house. Twin racks of guns laddered one end of the room, shotguns in one rack and rifles in another. A bar was across the opposite end; above the bar were three shelves of trophies—loving cups awarded the most inspirational player on his high school football team, the state broadjump champion, the All-Coast end, the Rose Bowl player. On a velvet pad were pinned a collection of gold and silver basketballs and footballs. A blown-up photo showed Gentry, helmetless, his teeth exposed in a smile, swiveling away from a Pittsburg tackler in the 1928 Rose Bowl game.

Standing before the bar as he poured drinks for his guests, Gentry looked as if he could still play ball. He weighed the hundred and eighty pounds he had carried into the Rose Bowl. His close-cut blond hair was little thinner, and it showed no gray. In repose his face seemed tired, but he could arouse himself at will and by sheer animal vitality, by the impact of his physical competence, dominate men of intelligence and experience.

Leadership came easy to Gentry. He accepted success as his due. In school, when sports were all important to him, he had matured early; a man among boys, he had always stood out. After college he had none of the athlete's usual difficulty in turning from sport to business. He loved competition: he always associated competition with victory. He played at business the way he played at football—to win, and he played rough. He enjoyed turning the rules to his own benefit. While older operators beefed about the uncertainty resulting from increased government controls, Gentry studied the laws and the administrators, estimated the changes they would make, decided where his competitors would entangle themselves in red tape, and moved swiftly to take advantage of a fluid situation. Even before he married Ruth Peterson, he was marked for success. And as manager of Peterson's empire he was as big as any little lumberman in the state—no Weyerhaeuser, but still important. He worked hard at being a success. He played along with the demand for sustained-yield forestry; he subsidized scientists to study wood plastics, and he followed a few of their suggestions; he bought ultra-modern machinery. The mill and the camps had larger pay rolls than ever, at a time when other lumber dynasties were edging toward disaster. Gentry built pay rolls. All he asked in return was to be allowed to make money and to keep on running things. In the beautiful house he had built on the hill, he was King of the Mountain. His worry was that someone might grow big enough to throw him off.

He passed the drinks. "I suppose you fellows know why I asked you up?"

Nobody denied it.

Englund said, "Have you seen him?"

"Our boy?"

"Yes."

"Yes, I've seen him."

"Well?"

"Steve says he didn't." Gentry looked at them over his drink. "I believe him."

The men looked at each other. Englund chewed on the butt of his cigar. Haines ran his finger inside his collar. Bob Kizer sat immobile in a leather chair, his fat legs stretched in front of him, only the rapid movement of his eyes from face to face betraying tension.

"It *was* Dawson then?" said Kizer.

"Steve thinks not. Dawson really was at a union meeting.

But what's important is that Steve broke in there last night. He found her dead. He admits that."

Englund said "Jesus Christ" around his cigar. Haines whistled softly. Kizer crossed his plump legs and sagged back into the receptive leather.

"Agreed," said Gentry. "And there's something else. Steve told me, and plenty damn late, that he was arrested a while back breaking into one of the union offices. Snow knows what he was doing. So does Bill Elliott."

"The Chief's all right," said Englund. "He'll play along."

"How about Elliott?"

Englund said, "Can't trust him."

Kizer asked, "Did Steve find anything on Dawson?"

"Nothing new. He cleared out when he saw the body."

Gentry let the information sink in, then went on. "So the situation is this. We don't know who killed her. It could have been Dawson, though that is improbable. And it could have been our man. The Chief knows our man was breaking into the house. If he wants to pin it on Steve, he can. And if he can't find anybody else and the unions start making it hot for him, that might happen."

"He better find somebody else," said Kizer. "He damn well better find somebody else."

Gentry went on. "My idea is this. We have some interesting information about Dawson. We had better turn it over to Jones. He can use it at the inquest to make a case against Dawson. Even if we can't get a true bill against him, we can make him look bad."

"What sort of information?"

"There was a gal he was sleeping with in Portland."

"That's a motive for murder," said Haines.

"Maybe his wife was a Catholic. Wouldn't give him a divorce."

Englund said, "What about Jones? Will he play ball?"

"He'll play ball," said Gentry. "He's all right."

"What about Elliott?"

"Something will have to be done about Elliott."

"What?"

"I don't know. We'd better check with the Chief on that. Bob, will you see Shaw? Find out if he has any strings on Elliott."

Kizer said, "Check."

Haines asked, "What about the paper?"

"What about it?"

"I mean, hadn't we better make sure the story is treated right?"

Gentry shook his head. "We don't want the *Logger* running any campaigns against Dawson."

"We don't?"

"That would be too obvious. We can let the coroner do his stuff, and the paper can run that as news. It'll look better that way. This is delicate. A wrong step and the public might get the wrong idea."

"Check, Gordon."

"Check."

"Check."

"All right, fellows. Let's go over it once. I turn our personal file on Dawson over to the coroner, and he uses the information to implicate Dawson in the murder. Bob, you see the Chief and make sure Elliott isn't going to blow things wide open by sounding off about Steve. And we all sit tight. Oh, yes—I'll see that the paper behaves itself. Agreed?"

Everyone agreed. ,

"And now," said Gentry, "about that Jamboree . . ."

The old man needed a drink. He so badly needed another

drink. There was liquor in town and he still had some money, but he didn't want to go to town. In town they might be after him. And it was a long way to town, and cold.

The fire had gone out, or he hadn't lit a fire—he couldn't remember whether it had gone out or he hadn't lit it—and it was cold in the shack. He picked up the bottles that lay beside the cot and shook them, but nothing gurgled. He smelled the bottles but found no pleasure in the sharp-sweet odor of vanilla and lemon extract. He needed that drink, needed it bad. *She's all right. Didn't hurt her at all. She's all right.* And he remembered the sound of the iron hitting her head, a dull, hollow sound. She hadn't screamed. Oh God, how he needed that drink. Then he remembered: he lurched over to the crate that served as cupboard and pulled out the sack of softening potatoes and reached in behind and brought out the thick-lidded, groove-sided can of canned heat. His hands shook so that he nicked himself with the icepick as he pried off the top. He looked around for a cloth, saw none, and picked up a sock. He scooped the gelatin out of the can, worked it into a lump in the heel of the sock, and squeezed the alcohol out into a cup. He drained the cup at a toss and shivered violently. *She's all right. Just a headache is all. All right.* He threw himself face down on the cot. Shudders racked him, but in a little while he felt better.

— VI —

NIGHT

THE lights were out on the business-office side; the accountant had gone home at five, the ad chasers at six, followed at eight by the society editor. Seward and the reporter and the sports editor had the editorial side to themselves.

Seward was editing the teletype copy, struggling to compress the national and international news into the scant space left by ads, features, editorials, comics, puzzles and local copy. His thoughts kept drifting from the news to Bill Elliott, and what Elliott would say when Seward changed his mind and wouldn't help; this wasn't pleasant to think about, and he tried not to, and, oddly, he found it easier to think about the Barovich girl, Steve's sister. She probably was Steve's sister, though he couldn't be sure. He'd asked Helene Lewis to describe the Barovich girl, and the phrase "beautiful in a Slavic sort of way" fitted. From the society editor he had also learned that her name was Monica, she lived at home, was unmarried, a Catholic, and seldom went out. But he could not fit her into the picture at Dawson's. The cop, Haarka, had mentioned other curiosity seekers who had been in earlier that night; there had been all the people on the front lawn. But why had she run? Why did she refuse to talk to him? And, living half a mile away, how had she learned so soon of the murder? Was it because she was Steve Barovich's sister? And that brought Seward back to Bill Elliott.

He turned his attention to the news.

Putting out the *Logger* was a job that paid him sixty-five dollars a week. It was a routine that took ten hours or more a day; a craft easy to learn and difficult to master; a contest with the editors of bigger and—well, of course—better papers in Portland.

But most of all, it was a game of solitaire in which the goal was his own conception of an Interesting Paper: the cards he played were the stories dealt by his reporters, the feature service and the news association; they came in several suits— sex, conflict, human interest—and their values were relative. A run of juicy sex stories increased the value of a political yarn as a change of pace; a series of hot international pieces could be aced by a simple boy-and-dog story. And, to a degree, the value of each story was subjective: Gale had spent a summer in Mexico, and Mexican items appeared in the *Logger;* he admired Ernest Hemingway, and though Cove had no bookstore and the library shelves were burdened by only one Hemingway book, *For Whom the Bell Tolls,* he made sure that *Logger* readers got to see every item that came over the wire about the lives and wives of America's hairiest author. But primarily, Seward's values were the values of every editor in the country. Each morning the *Logger* looked like the other small-town papers of the same day, and as much like the metropolitan papers as mechanical limitations would permit. He judged his paper by the papers he had seen; and the perfect edition he hoped to put out was a composite of the features he liked best in other papers—the San Francisco *Chronicle's* use of pictures; the New York *Herald Tribune's* writing and editorial judgment; the Los Angeles *Times'* typography; the *Daily News'* sour approach to social reporting. Above all, his aim was interest.

Yet tonight, with a story that had everything—sex, conflict, human interest, local personalities—he felt dissatisfied. He was glad when Thomas, the backshop foreman, called in his high, complaining voice, "Time, time everybody."

At ten-thirty the backshop gang knocked off for lunch, and

Seward usually joined them. One group of printers and typographers gathered behind the press, took their lunches out of paper bags, and talked of the farms they intended to retire to, the lottery they hoped to win, the price of eggs, and, tonight, of the murder. The rest of the printers went out to lunch, not always by-passing the beer parlors on their way down the street to the Goal Line or the Greek's.

MacIntyre stopped by Seward's desk. "Coming, Gale?"

"I'll be along in a couple minutes. Order me a hamburger."

"Okay." Mac went out, hitching his cork leg along with a full swing of his body.

Seward finished editing the UN story for the day. He checked to see there was enough copy to keep the linotypes busy for a while after they resumed operation; he copied the Coast League baseball scores (he always took the scores to the Goal Line, which ran a baseball pool) and then he went out, leaving the editorial offices to Joe Kalinen, who was sitting in a corner, hat on the back of his head, writing the murder story and drinking gin out of a coke bottle—every inch a Hollywood reporter.

The night was dark, but the air was clear. The clouds stretched solidly across the valley from mountain top to mountain top, and there was neither moon nor stars. But below the clouds the lights of the town sparkled and the air smelled sharply of forest and sea.

"Hey, Gale." Bill Elliott was standing behind the latticework that connected a pair of billboards on the vacant lot next to the *Logger* building. He motioned.

Seward walked over to him, circling the billboard. He felt guilty about letting Elliott down, and his discomforture turned to annoyance at the big cop. "For Christ sake, Bill, why the cops and robber stuff? You could have come into the office."

"I thought you wanted to protect your reputation as an

editorial virgin," Elliott said, piqued by Seward's tone. "People might talk if they saw us together."

"Oh, balls."

"What's the matter?"

"I don't go for this stuff."

"What stuff don't you go for?"

"Look, Bill, I've been thinking over that business of last night, and I've got no call to go conspiring against public officials. The mayor, the council, the Chief, any of them."

"Oh."

"If you want to make trouble for them, go ahead. I'm not going to tip them off, and I'll give you a fair shake on any stories that come out of it. But I'm not going to enter into any conspiracy."

"Even a conspiracy of silence." Elliott checked himself. "No, sorry, I didn't mean that, Gale. But what's gone wrong? You talk to the Boss about this?"

"No, I haven't talked to the Boss about this."

"What have you got to lose?"

"That's not the point."

"What *is* the point?"

Seward shook his head. "I don't want to argue about it, Bill. I just can't do it."

Elliott said, "I'm all set to get up and blow the lid off things at the next council meeting."

"If you do, I'll print it. I just don't want to be involved in advance."

"That's fair enough," Elliott said, his voice tight.

"I think so."

"Jesus, you sit in there and you get the news of the whole goddam world every night on that ticker, lots more news than most people get to see, and you're paid to read the whole works, and you get it first, before ninety-nine out of a hundred see it, and it still doesn't add up for you. It's all in pieces. You're so damn interested in stories you don't even know what's going on. You don't want to be involved in advance, for Christ sake. Since when aren't you involved? Who the hell are you—the man from Mars? The walking dead? Don't want to be involved!"

"Oh, balls." He didn't feel like sermons, he told himself, except when he'd had half a gallon of wine. "You go make some news and I'll print it. The same for the Chief."

"I'll make you some news all right."

In anger and disappointment, the two men moved apart.

MacIntyre was waiting at the Goal Line. "Your hamburger's cold," he said.

"My fault. I got held up." Seward slid onto the stool. The waiter came over and Seward gave him the slip with the baseball results. The waiter looked at them, whistled, and said, "Those lousy Beavers—twelve runs. That beats me." He went to a blackboard and chalked the scores into the inning frames.

Seward ate his hamburger. It was cold, all right; he was sick of hamburgers, sick of quick lunches, sick of sitting on a stool and eating off a greasy counter. He felt Mac's eyes on him and he deliberately finished his sandwich without looking around at the printer.

"I've paid for it," Mac said when he finished.

He fished in his watch pocket for change, but Mac shook his head. "Your turn tomorrow."

"Thanks."

They went out onto the street.

"Anything wrong?"

Seward shook his head.

"Anything new on the story?"

"Oh, Christ, Mac, I'm all mixed up."

"It's quite a story," Mac said quietly. "It's got a lot of angles. A lot of angles."

They went back to the office in silence, and Seward felt a great warmness toward the crippled printer.

— VII —

THE INQUEST

THE council chamber, where the inquest was to be held, was long, narrow and comfortable. In front of the rail was a U-shaped desk, bordered by leather-padded swivel chairs; back of the rail were eight rows of theater-type seats. "Nothing," Mayor Everett had told the architect, "is more important than making sure our citizens can sleep through council meetings." Engravings of George Washington, Harry Truman and Abraham Lincoln looked glumly down from the wall. A furled flag stood in a corner. The floor had been swept with oiled sawdust and the room had an unmistakable public-building odor.

Except for the coroner, nobody was in the chamber. Xenophon Jones hummed as he walked about the room on the balls of his feet. Three times he rehearsed the entrance he would make: he would come in briskly, walk to the closed end of the desk, lay his brief case on the chair, put the box with the steam iron on the desk, pull on a pair of white gloves and, quite deliberately, take the iron from the box. That would be effective. He wondered if he should open the inquest with a salute to the flag.

He was a solidly built man, square of chin, firm of mouth, and bald except for a narrow half-circle of gray hair that gave him the appearance of having a horseshoe wrapped around the back of his head. His eyes were small, pale blue and so wide-set they seemed to operate independently. His heavy jaw was freshly shaved and powdered but still showed

a shadow. He wore a dark, double-breasted suit. His movements were studied, dignified and faintly comical.

In the early days of the community he had served as the
lumber-company doctor. Eventually the state checked on
his credentials. (He blamed the I. W. W. for the investigation
and complained to friends: "The Wobblies are out to break
all respectable people.") After abandoning his medical practice at the state's request, he turned undertaker—an occupa-
tional shift that amused the townsfolk. He never replied to
their sallies about the possibility that as a doctor he had prepared the ground for a bumper crop of customers for his
later profession. But once, when lampooned at a businessman's luncheon, he broke into tears. He did not go to another meeting for more than a year, and when he did there
was no more heckling. In time, his peculiar antecedents
were so familiar they were no longer mentioned, which was
almost as good as being forgotten.

He was not unpopular—his funerals were the cheapest
in town—and when early in the depression he found himself in financial difficulties and filed for coroner, he was the
only Republican elected in the county. (That was the year
Senator Olson came back home to devote his full time to
journalism.) Though they turned their dead over to more
modern undertakers—men who called themselves morticians
and advertised on the radio and outlined their establish-
ments in pale neon—the people of Cove continued to re-
elect Xenophon Jones coroner. He sometimes thought of
running for higher office, but always the fear of defeat kept
him from filing.

As he rehearsed now, he thought of himself as Prosecuting
Attorney Jones.

At noon he walked back to the undertaking parlors. A
misty rain was falling and he had no topcoat, but he walked
springily on the balls of his feet, humming as he went.

A woman was sitting in the waiting room. He paused to arrange his dignity; then, seeing it was Nellie, he said, "Oh, it's you."

"Yes, it's me."

"Would you mind coming back tomorrow? I have a great deal to attend to."

"What's the matter, Doc? Don't you like money?"

He sighed and opened the office door. "All right. Come in here." Cove had an unofficial licensing system for prostitutes. Every girl was required to take a physical examination twice a month; each examination cost the harlot twenty dollars, of which Jones kept five and city officials got the rest. The system kept the venereal rate down; it was almost legal, quite profitable and attracted little attention. When the system was originated, Jones had all the girls come in at the same time for their examination. That proved to be a mistake. Not only did the horde of women streaming into the undertaking establishment on alternate Mondays seem strange to Jones's neighbors, but the girls from rival houses sometimes quarreled, and once the Reverend Mr. Devin, the Baptist minister, had to shout a funeral sermon so that it could be heard above the uproar of Jones's more lively customers. Since then the girls had individual appointments.

He examined Nellie perfunctorily. "You're okay."

"Doc?"

"What?"

"A guy bit me the other day, here." Her hand went to her breast. "Doc, is that likely to give me—" she hesitated before the word—"cancer?"

"It could if it happened often enough."

"Well, not very often. But could you sort of check now? Could you tell already if it's going to be?"

"That's not my line."

"But couldn't you look?"

"No. I'm very busy. I suggest you see a doctor."

"You're not very helpful."

She paid him, cash, and left. She walked slowly back to Snug Harbor through rain that was now falling hard, and she wished to Christ there was someone she could talk to.

In his office, Jones studied the file of material on Bull Dawson that Gentry had sent him. Except for the report of a private detective who had followed Dawson during the five days of a union convention in Portland, the file had little.

He read the detective's report again, carefully.

Spectators began arriving shortly after one o'clock. The first-comers were old-age pensioners, who had time to kill; they came early and read Townsend literature and talked quietly among themselves, calling each other Mister. They were followed by housewives and a few high school kids, then by a group of men from the union, all wearing their Sunday suits, with blue and white union buttons on the lapels.

The policemen who were to testify came in together at a quarter to two and lounged against the wall on the official side of the railing. Joe Kalinen arrived drunk, a roll of copy paper sticking from his coat pocket like a swollen cigar; he took one of the seats at the official table, spread his paper before him and pretended to take notes; several times he went to the lavatory, where he took a draw from the pint in his coat pocket. Rutherford Olson came in, paused in the doorway to bow very slightly to the crowd, and took the seat next to Kalinen. When Gale Seward came in, he saw his boss and reporter together; he nodded hello, but went to sit by the cops. By a quarter to two all the seats back of the rail were taken. The room smelled of wet clothing.

Dawson came in a few minutes before two, flanked by Plotch and Toivenen. He was wearing his leather jacket; his pants were unpressed and muddy at the cuffs; the rain had darkened his brown hair and plastered it low on his forehead. Stubble dirtied his cheeks. His eyes were dull and veined with red. He looked vaguely at the spectators for a long moment, then saw a vacant seat toward the back of the room and started for it. Plotch caught him gently by the arm and steered him to a chair at the council table.

Joe Kalinen came over and said, "Any statement for the press, Bull?" He said it loud enough for the last row of spectators to hear.

"You're bucking for a busted ass."

Kalinen, grinning, walked away.

Plotch put his head close to Dawson's. "Take it easy, Bull; you got to keep your head."

"Okay."

"You shouldn't have got drunk."

"Okay."

"What would have happened if we hadn't found you? You got to think of that."

"Okay."

"Christ, Bull, I know how you needed it, but you shouldn't have gone to that speak."

"Okay."

Plotch's lean face pulled away out of focus, but Toivenen's came at him through the mist of nausea and alcohol. "Let me call the lawyer, Bull."

"No."

"It's not for you to say. It's not just you they want to crucify, Bull, it's the movement. You're in no shape to take care of yourself if Jonesey gets cute."

"I'm all right."

"You look like the green end of duck crap. God almighty, man, let me get our lawyer."

"You do and I'll beat hell out of you."

And Toivenen's big bony face pulled away.

Dawson leaned forward on his arms. All he wanted was to be let alone, to sleep. He had lain in bed for hours trying to sleep, fighting against thought, and early in the morning he had dressed and walked to the bootlegger's. That was all. He'd gone to the bootlegger's and bought a bottle and finished it there. And he had gone right to sleep. He'd been asleep when Toivenen and Plotch found him. Jesus god, but it was good to sleep. To sleep, to be let alone, that wasn't a hell of a lot to ask. Not to have anyone else say, "I know how you feel, but. . ." when they couldn't know how he felt, and the *but* always was an argument that he ought to do something. He didn't want to do anything but forget. He settled his head into the crook of his elbow. The top of the table felt cool on his chin. The nausea ebbed away and the world steadied.

The spectators stirred; there was a scuffling of feet, a pause in the conversations. Dawson raised his head. Xenophon Jones had bustled in. He was arranging his papers at the head of the table. Dawson squinted at him through burning eyelids. The coroner was a moving blur.

The proceedings flowed around him, a stream of words, words that ran on and on, as meaningless as the brown waters of the Tala. Some of the time he dozed with his arms folded on the desk and let the stream flow over him, and some of the time he strained to see to the bottom of the torrent, but could not. The coroner's jury was selected, the cause of death stated, the bloodstained iron exhibited (he did not look), and the testimony of the police procedure on the case was taken. Then, abruptly, Xenophon Jones was standing beside him, a hand on his shoulder. He straightened and looked up at the coroner. The heavy, round face was bunched in a sympathetic smile. "I must ask you a few questions,

Mr. Dawson. Simply a matter of form. I know how you must feel, but. . ."

"Yes," Dawson said, "I know."

"Your name?"

"William C. Dawson."

"What does the C stand for?"

"Nothing. Just C."

"Oh. In what country were you born?"

Dawson looked at him sharply, the silliness of the question piercing the shell of torpor. "This country."

"In this country. You're an American then?"

"Yes."

"You're sure."

"Yes." Suddenly he was angry. "Right here in Cove," he shouted. "Nineteen fourteen. Want to see my draft card?"

"No, that won't be necessary. What nationality were your parents?"

"I don't know."

"You don't know!"

"Well, American, of course. Dad's folks were Scotch-Irish, I guess. They'd been in the country since hellangone, and mother's side was Swedish. Came over during the Civil War, or about that time." It was a long speech and it made his head ache. He closed his eyes and rubbed the heel of his hand across his forehead.

"What is your profession, Dawson?"

"I'm a logger."

"A logger is all?"

"Yes."

"You don't work for a union?"

"I'm a union official, but it's a union of loggers."

"And that makes you a logger?"

"Yes."

"You use the term loosely. I would say you are a labor leader."

"All right."

"You admit you're not a logger?"

"No."

"But you admit you're a labor leader?"

"Yes."

"What led you to become a labor leader?"

He had been answering the questions automatically, responding without thought, barely conscious of the hostility in the words that issued from the round, smiling face. But now he paused. What *had* made him become a labor leader? He had not always been one, nor had he ever consciously wanted to be one. He could remember the time when he wanted to be a doctor: there had been no money. Instead of college he had shipped on a halibut boat; it was wrecked on the Alaskan coast and for a time he was stranded in Juneau, where he earned his passage by working on a relief project, redecorating Tlingit Totem poles. After getting back to Cove, he went to work in the woods, slinging rigging. When the big drive to organize the loggers started, he joined early. He remembered the organizer who got him: Red Hanson, a big, dumb, tough Swede who'd been around for years and said he'd known Joe Hill. Hanson still carried his Wobbly card and he carried scars on his back from running the gantlet of deputies at Everett. Hanson had said, "I figured it out a long time ago, kid, and all it comes down to is, us against the bastards. You're either with us or with them." And he had signed.

The coroner repeated, impatiently, "How did you happen to become a labor leader?"

"Ah, I don't know."

"You are president of your local union and you don't know why you are a labor leader?"

"Yes."

"Could it be because you believe in violence?"

The question jarred him. The shimmering screen that had stood between him and the world dissolved. He looked around the narrow, coffin-like room, at the spectators whose faces were centered on him—white masks of sympathy or hostility or curiosity; at Leo Plotch on his right, a long, anxious face; at Arne Toivenen, whose bulging eyes glared violence at the coroner; at Joe Kalinen, writing rapidly on a pad of folded paper; at Xenophon Jones, who still smiled fatly down at him.

And looking into the coroner's round, friendly face, he was abruptly aware of danger. The danger shocked him and left him shaken and sick. They were trying to pin Dee's death on him. He was cold with fear, then hot with anger. "Dirty bastard," he blurted, "goddam dirty bastard."

Toivenen kicked him sharply in the ankle and he stopped swearing.

Jones said smoothly, "I understand that you must be under severe strain, Mr. Dawson, and I will make allowances." He paused, then asked softly, "Do you often give way to violence?"

"No."

"Not often?"

"Never."

"You do not believe in violence?"

"No."

"You are a labor leader and you do not believe in violence?"

"That's right."

"What if strikebreakers try to cross a line?"

"They got to be stopped."

"Non-violently?"

Dawson said carefully, "A man has a right to use any

means to protect his home against intrusion, and I feel he has an equal right to protect his job from some strikebreaking fink."

"By use of violence?"

"I'm not a pacifist. A man can use violence to protect his home." He stopped and waited until he was sure his voice would be steady. "If I had been home the other night, I'd have resisted whoever it was."

"You believe in violence if the provocation is great enough."

"Yes."

"And you, yourself, are the one to determine the amount of provocation?"

His head was throbbing and he had a helpless, dreamlike impression of being strait-jacketed in a burning house. Looking into the coroner's small, wide-set eyes he remembered a day long before, in the high school gym, when he had put on the gloves with a boy who fought professionally: he remembered the helplessness of knowing the pug was going to knock him out and yet not being able to stop him, of having no adequate way of resisting; and the fighter had knocked him out with a short left when he was watching for a right.

"I believe in self-defense."

"An eye for an eye?"

"If you want to put it that way."

"And you got to be president of your union because you are a rough, tough guy who will slug it out with the mill owners, using violence if necessary?"

"Hell, no." It was almost funny how he had entered union politics. In high school he had taken typing and for several months he had helped out in the union office, typing reports. In those months he learned the principles of organization. He was a natural: he knew the men in the woods, he knew the work, he knew organization; further, he was anti-boss.

When he ran for vice-president he was overwhelmingly elected, and when the president of the local took over a post in the national organization Bull inherited the office. He worked hard at being president and looked on the post as a career; it was like any other job: if you came through for the boss, you got ahead—though in his case the boss was the loggers in the woods. If he maneuvered the loggers into a position to get better pay and better working conditions, he might be promoted. But it wasn't quite the same as working for a company. Always there was the idea he shared with Red Hanson—*us against the bastards*. "They made me president because I can type."

The hint of laughter among the spectators angered Jones. He feared laughter. "I must warn you, sir, not to obstruct justice."

Dawson lurched to his feet. The crowd made a sudden, collective sound at his movement and he paused, aware of his disheveled appearance: his beard, his unpressed clothes, his matted hair. Momentarily he tugged at the cuffs of his shirt. Then he shrugged off the desire to be neat and his eyes leveled on the coroner. "Obstruct justice, for Christ sake. I just want to remind you that I have a greater interest in seeing justice done than you can possibly have. I came here to answer questions that will help you find who killed her, and I'm damned if you've got any right to push me around because I happen to be president of a union."

From behind the rail one of the spectators shouted, "Yesus, Bull, that's telling him."

Jones walked to the rail. His face was white and his hands shook. "If there is any further disturbance I shall ask the police to clear the chamber."

Toivenen tugged at Dawson's sleeve. "Shall I get the lawyer?"

"Yeah."

Toivenen got up and whispered to Plotch, "If he gets Bull on the run, stall till I get back." Plotch nodded, and Toivenen went through the swinging doors, down the linoleum padded steps and out into the rain, while in the room he had left the inquisition went on.

"You were the last person known to have seen your wife alive and the first to see her dead, Dawson. It is only natural that we should want to question you about your attitude toward violence."

"Why, you—"

Jones' tight smile of triumph stopped him. He waited, gulping at the knot that clogged his throat. When he spoke he spoke so gently that his voice did not carry beyond the rail. "Don't do this. Don't do this."

Jones trumpeted, "Don't threaten me, sir. I will not be intimidated by threats."

Plotch was holding Dawson's wrist and dragged him down onto a chair. Dawson said, loud this time, "Do you realize what you're doing?" Did he realize this frame-up was a declaration of war? That the fight would be uglier than the peace that preceded it.

"I'm conducting an investigation into the death of your wife." He paused and stood looking at Dawson out of his wide-spaced little eyes, "You loved your wife?"

You son-of-a-bitch, he thought. But he said, "What do you think?"

"I have no preconceptions."

"I loved her."

"And you never quarreled?"

"No."

"How long were you married?"

"Nine years."

"And in all that time you never quarreled?"

"No more than usual, I guess."

"But you did quarrel."

"Oh, some."

"Why did you say you didn't?"

"I didn't think that's what you meant."

"You didn't understand the word quarrel?"

"Yes, but I thought you meant more than usual."

"How much is usual?"

"I don't know. Not much."

"But you did quarrel some?"

"Nothing serious."

"What do you consider serious?"

"No blows."

"You quarreled, but always stopped short of hitting her?"

"I never came close to hitting her."

"Not even when she found out about Helen Morrinson?"

There it was again. You watch for the right that can knock you out, and the left catches you flush, square, and leaves you a set-up for the right.

"Helen Morrinson," Dawson repeated the name in a dull voice. "Helen Morrinson."

Jones pressed his advantage. "You remember her?"

"Yes."

"Where did you meet her?"

"Portland."

"When?"

"At the convention."

"What convention?"

"Our convention. Last September." He was aware that Plotch was looking at him strangely, and he got a spasm of satisfaction that Helen Morrinson was something even Leo Plotch didn't know about.

"You were in love with her?"

"No."

"But you made love to her?"

"No." It was his first false testimony, but he could see no alternative.

Jones let him wait for the next one. "You met her on September twelfth?"

"I don't remember the date."

"You met her on September twelfth." It was a statement this time, not a question. "You met her on the afternoon of the twelfth. You had dinner with her at the Multanomah, and you spent the night in her apartment. And the next night."

It was true, of course; it was true as hell. He had met Helen between sessions at the convention. She was a tall girl with a potatoish face but a good body, fine legs, and a passion for unionism that extended to union men. They talked union talk for hours, over dinner, over beer at a tavern, over whiskey at her apartment, and when it was time for him to go there had been no need for him to go, and he stayed. It had meant nothing except that she was willing and he was away from home. He had not thought of Helen Morrinson more than a couple of times since. But how could he talk about it before a crowd of people, who, like himself, disapproved of adultery, whether they practiced it or not. He could no more talk about it in this courtroom, before these people, than he could take off his clothes.

"You were in love with Helen Morrinson, and your wife stood in the way. She was Catholic and wouldn't give you a divorce."

"No. She wasn't Catholic. She was Lutheran."

"But she wouldn't give you a divorce."

"I didn't want one."

"I suggest you did."

And that was the phrase Bull could not bear. All the anger and hurt and frustration and numbness and bewilderment of the enduring hours since Dee's death came to a head in the words, *I suggest you did*. He was suggesting so much more than a talk about divorce, a talk that had never taken place; he was suggesting a murder that had most awfully been committed, and a murderer who . . . Dawson wanted this done with, completed, over. He wanted no more questions. And the way to stop questions was to pound a fist into the broad, heavy, wide-eyed face from which the dirty questions streamed.

But Plotch moved first.

"Mr. Jones," Plotch said, rising from his chair, unfolding slowly to his lean six-feet-two, "I have something to say."

The coroner diverted his attention from Dawson. He looked awkwardly up at the man towering over him. "You are out of order."

Leo Plotch talked on over the interruption. "All right. I'm out of order. It is easy to be out of order. You try to help your fellowman and you're out of order. But if you persecute him, nail him to a cross, rub salt in his wounds, twist the knife, apply the lash, steal the bread, befoul the water, then you are in order, in order with conformity and regulation and all the corruption of which our world stinks. You are in order. You are in the great tradition."

"You are in contempt."

"I am in contempt. Yes. I am filled with contempt, pressed down, running over. I am in contempt of court, if this be a court. My contempt runneth over. This man," and he bent his head toward Bull, who was staring at the brown linoleum floor, "has lost his wife. The night she was killed, I was with Bull Dawson. Others were with him. But you do not even try to establish where he was. Instead, you insinuate the vileness of your own festering mind. You impute evil where goodness exists. You pervert a man's disaster and distress, you besmirch the memory of a fine woman, you desecrate a love. And for what? For thirty pieces of silver? For a nice fat check from Gordon Gentry at election time? For—"

"Arrest that man."

"Are you such a fool that you do not think the people will know? Or are you getting so much that you don't care?"

The cops were coming toward him, two of them, grinning amiably. The spectators were on their feet, angry and uncertain, held from action by the conventions of courtroom behavior. Plotch knew he could goad them into action with a few more words, but he hesitated. His outburst was premeditated, a deliberate attempt to take the pressure off Dawson before Bull exploded into foolish action or admission, a stall for time until Toivenen returned with the lawyer. It would do more harm than good to start a riot.

As the police took his arms, one on each side, Plotch twisted toward the crowd. "Easy does it, fellows. Don't let Jonesey trick you into anything foolish. He's nothing but Gentry's pratt-boy anyway."

One of the cops—the Finn, Haarka,—said, "Come on Leo, let's go down and make speeches for the desk sergeant, huh?"

"What am I charged with?"

"What's he charged with, Jonesey?"

"Contempt of court. Obstructing justice. Inciting to riot."

The cop said, "Disorderly conduct." He led Plotch out of the room, guiding him with a hand on his elbow. On the steps they met Toivenen and the lawyer, Al Addison, both panting and wet from running through the rain.

"What the hell?" Toivenen asked, his pop eyes going from Plotch to the cop and back.

"I created a disorder," said Plotch. "Our lovely pal Jonesey was being nasty. He's found out that Bull made some gal in Portland at the last convention, and he's trying to say Bull knocked off Dee so he could marry her. I made a speech to sort of take everybody's mind off it."

The cop said, "Pretty good speech, too. You sounded like Churchill used to on the radio."

"Hell," said Plotch, "I sounded like that when Winston was still a reporter. Haven't you ever heard it said that Churchill sounds like Plotch?" He turned to Toivenen, who was not amused. "Anyway, Jonesey got off the track long enough to have me arrested for inciting to mutiny and impersonating Zola. You'd better get on up there. He's got Bull on the run."

"What about you?" Toivenen asked, starting up the stairs.

"I'll be okay. Fine, or a few days in jail, depending on how the police judge feels. It was worth it. You should have seen Jones. Fit to pop a hernia."

Toivenen went up the steps with the lawyer in tow. Al Addison was a man of fifty-odd years, with bold, clean features and a fine head of close-cropped graying hair. He had started considering himself a liberal during the days of Wilson's New Freedom, and he followed in the footsteps of the reformers as they appeared: LaFollette, Roosevelt, Wallace. He somehow maintained the friendship if not the respect of the conservatives of the community; he might even had had their respect if he had ever managed to amass money, but he never did. He represented so many local unions that he once told Plotch, "Jurisdictionals give me schizophrenia." He liked Bull Dawson and was angry with himself for not having come to the inquest without being asked. He followed Toivenen into the courtroom.

Jones was standing beside Dawson, who looked beat out. "When you talked about a divorce," Jones was saying, "did you have one of your quarrels?"

Addison said, "He doesn't have to answer that.'

Jones turned to face Addison. He was still upset after Plotch's outburst, and though he had expected a lawyer to be present at the inquest, he was not prepared for one to appear at this moment. Addison came through the gate in the rail and took Plotch's seat beside Dawson. "Don't say anything more, Bull, without talking to me."

"This bastard's trying to frame me."

Jones pulled himself together. "This is an inquest, not a trial. The defendant—I mean, the witness does not have the need, or the right, to be represented by counsel."

"No? Prove that."

"The burden of proof is not on me. If you wish to get an injunction—"

"And in the meantime let you spread your poison."

"I have already declared one man in contempt today."

"You have no right to do that. You are not a judge."

"My duty is to investigate the cause of death. I must ask you not to interfere."

"You cannot deny the right of counsel."

Jones looked around the room for another policeman. Elliott was standing against the wall by the door. The coroner motioned for him, and Elliott moved across the room and took his place beside the coroner.

"If this man interferes in any way, book him for contempt," Jones said to Elliott.

Addison said, "This is not a court."

"You are in contempt," said Jones. And to Elliott, "Arrest this man."

Elliott said, "There is something I want to say about this business."

"Arrest that man," Jones shouted. "Arrest him, I say. Arrest him."

Chief Snow lurched from his seat at the far side of the table and came around to Jones. "Look, Doc," he said "we'll arrest him if you want, but I sort of think Al's right. You can't arrest a lawyer just for making like a lawyer. Not and make it stick, you can't. And false arrest is sort of messy. Why don't you call it a day? You can continue the hearing tomorrow."

"The funeral's tomorrow."

"Day after, then. Look, Doc, it's for the best." He had his hand on Jones's shoulder and he emphasized his words by nodding slowly. "It's for the best," he repeated. "Declare a recess."

"The day after tomorrow will be fine with us," Addison said. "Make it the day after tomorrow." He was looking speculatively at Elliott.

"All right," Jones said, looking in bewilderment from Addison to Snow to Elliott, wondering what had gone wrong. He rapped his knuckles on the table, hitting the wood beside Dawson, who, slumped in his chair showed no interest. "The inquest is recessed until the day after tomorrow."

— VIII —

RIPTIDE

GALE SEWARD left the courtroom with the crowd. He wanted to hear what they were saying. Even more, he wanted not to talk to Olson or Joe Kalinen; he did not want to hear what they thought about the proceedings. He felt sick, drained. It was the feeling he had known in his freshman days after watching the college team take a beating. And, recognizing the feeling, he was angry with himself. There should be special ways to feel disappointment.

The spectators weren't saying much. Those Gale could hear were talking about Plotch or about Helen Morrinson. They said little about Jones. They had seen so much and they did not have things figured out; the incidents had not resolved themselves into a comprehensible total.

The crowd milled inside the glass doors leading to the street. They were adjusting raincoats, getting umbrellas half-cocked, watching the rain slant across the panes. Seward stood with them, wondering if he should go down to the basement and see Plotch. That wasn't his job—Kalinen was supposed to be the reporter—but there was only one way to be sure the *Logger* would get the story straight. He was edging toward the door to the police station when he saw the girl. She had been carrying her raincoat and her hair was braided and he had not recognized her, but as she slipped on the red raincoat he realized she was Monica Barovich. He shouldered through the crowd and said, "I didn't expect to see you here."

She looked her surprise, but said nothing. After tying

the white scarf over her head, carefully, ignoring him, she pushed open the glass door and went out into the rain. He walked beside her. "Going home?"

Monica Barovich did not answer. She walked in the direction of the bridge. The rain fell steadily, a solid rain that could fall for days. Seward felt it soaking into his clothes. "What's the matter? Don't you like newspapermen?"

She lengthened her stride and walked on, her eyes squinted against the rain, water beading on the strands of hair that poked from under the scarf. She looked very Slavic. He liked her looks and hated her composure; he wanted to learn what she knew. "You going to let them frame Bull?" he asked, on an impulse.

Monica Barovich kept on walking, but she looked up at him, a long look that told him nothing except that she had gray eyes. Her lips were drawn across her teeth and her high Slavic cheekbones emphasized the strain in her face. Abruptly she stopped and said, "It would be perhaps better if we went some place where we could talk."

"It would indeed," he said. He had not intended to mock her rather formal English, and he hastened to add, "The choice is limited, though. There are a lot of people in the *Logger* office, probably. That leaves my place, your place, or a restaurant. How about the Greek's?"

"Do you have a car?"

"No, but I can borrow one at the office."

She nodded. They crossed the street and walked to the *Logger* plant. They walked in silence. The advertising manager's Olsmobile was parked in front of the building. Gale opened the office door, leaned in and said, "Can I borrow the jalopy for an hour, Vince? I'm on a story."

"Take it away. The keys are in it." Vince was leaning over the counter, adding up column inches of advertising. "Tight paper tomorrow, Gale."

Out of gratitude for the loan of the car, the city editor did not remark that the paper was always full of ads on days when there was news.

He closed the door, shook his head to himself, and helped Monica into the Olds. The door on the driver's side was locked and she opened it for him from the inside. He fumbled for the starter, jerked the car badly in backing out, but by the time he reached the road that ran along the shore of the cove he was driving smoothly and feeling pleasure at the sure power under his right foot. They drove in silence past the white ramparts of the plywood plant and out into the ravaged stumplands. Each looked at the wet, blurred world through separate wedges cut by the beating windshield wiper.

After a time he said, "I'm Gale Seward. I'm city editor of the paper."

She said, "Oh." Just a polite *Oh* that was a receipt for information rather than an acknowledgment of surprise. That was all she said. He thought about ways of phrasing questions but could decide on none he thought would get answers, so he said nothing either: he just drove.

The road ran with few curves through the wasteland of stumps; it curved up a hill that in some countries would have been called a mountain, and dropped down to the dune-lands. As always, the Pacific came as a surprise, appearing suddenly between a gap in the dunes, spread endlessly westward. Today the ocean lowered under the beating rain, a sullen gray mass stretching to a near horizon.

At the ocean, Seward turned south and followed a graveled road to the top of a knoll overlooking the cove bar. The road ended there, and he stopped the car between two picnic tables. He twisted in the seat so that he was almost facing the girl, but she stared out of the side window, which was less rain-streaked, at the small waves that collapsed into froth along the line of the bar.

"Slack tide," he said, almost to himself. "No wind. And the rain's keeping the waves down."

"I hate it," she said, still looking out the window.

"The rain?"

"The rain. The ocean. All of it." She watched them for a time, the rain and ocean she hated. Then she said with an odd defiance, "I was born on the Adriatic."

"*Dobar dan.*"

She turned and studied him with gray eyes. "*Govorite li Hrvat?*"

"I only speak it a little," he replied, in English.

"But your name isn't. . ." she hesitated.

"My name isn't Croatian? Gale Seward. I changed it from Srdovich."

"Really?"

"No, not really. That's a personal gag. I roomed with two Croatian football players at the U—Lazar and Petrovich. They talked Croatian all the time, and I picked it up. A little." Disappointment showed in her face, so he added, "I've read a lot about Yugoslavia. What part of the Adriatic are you from?"

"Split. I was born there. Why do you read about Croatia?"

"It's my vice. I like books better than people."

"So do I. Is that bad?"

"I don't know. A professor I had once at the U, a journalism prof, said it was bad. It was just one of those odd remarks that somebody makes, not thinking, and they stick with you. I've always felt a little guilty about being a bookworm, since then." He paused to think it over; he decided what he had said was true, and not merely conversation based on truth, and so he changed the subject. "You like Split better than Cove?"

"Yes. Does that surprise you?"

"No. Should it?"

She didn't answer, and he asked, "It never rains in Split?"

"It rains, but the country is not raw and the city is old and beautiful, very beautiful, and the people live with grace even if they have not much money. The buildings are made of stone and brick, not of wood. The wood is left in the trees, and the trees are standing. Here everything is so new and raw you feel exposed. The roots here do not go deep. I wake in the night when the wind is blowing and think that perhaps in the morning there will be no town; it will be all cut down and blown away like the trees. There is no history, there are no roots. I like Split better."

He looked out through the windshield, evenly blurred now that the engine was off and the wiper not running. A troller was approaching the channel slowly, bucking the outgoing tide.

"I rather like it," he said, "but I guess it's all what you grow up with. I like the feeling of being able to drive a few miles and look at something that hasn't changed since the first Spaniard looked at it."

"First Englishman," she corrected him.

"No, first Spaniard. The Spanish were first. They came up from Mexico. Then the English, the Americans, the Russians, and even some Frenchmen. I've read their logs. Every one of them complains about our rain, even the Russians who came down from Sitka, where it really rains." He paused and watched the troller as it swung through the tricky passage in the bar and entered the protection of the cove. "I don't mind the rain, but I'd swap the city hall for Diocletian's palace, any day," he concluded, getting the conversation back to Split.

"I don't like the city hall," she said, picking up a different cue. "What did you think of the inquest?"

And there they were, face to face with the thing that had brought them together.

"It's not my dish."

"You do not like inquests?"

"Not this one."

"Why not this one?"

"It wasn't an inquest, it was a trial. Jonesey had the idea he was a prosecuting attorney."

"They are not all like this one?"

"Not by a damn sight. Even without Plotch flipping his lid the way he did, this one was different. Like a bad apple is different."

"How was it different?"

"Ordinarily they aren't trying to frame anybody."

She took a long time thinking that over, so long that he was afraid she was on another silence strike. But at last she said, "You do not think Dawson murdered his wife?"

"In the immortal words of Coroner Xenophon Jones, I have no preconceptions," he said bitterly. "No, I don't think he killed her. For that matter, neither does Jones."

"You are sure?"

"That Jones doesn't think he killed her? Yes, I'm sure."

The realization that the inquest was a frame-up was still strong upon him; it made him sick. He had not tried to put his thoughts into words and sentences, to arrange the ideas that raced through his mind while Jones was talking: he had not even thought of doing so; there had been no time for that. He had merely listened to Jones and there had come to him the sure, poisonous knowledge of what was being perpetrated.

She said, "Why?"

"At an inquest all the coroner has to do is show that somebody died an unnatural death," he said, going back to the beginning. "So Jones really didn't have much work to do. All he had to do was prove that Dee Dawson didn't die a natural death, and that shouldn't tax even Jones's abilities.

But what does he do instead? He goes Paul Muni on us. He puts on this exhibition of a district attorney saving the pee-pul from God knows what."

Seward paused, and thought about what he had said. He watched the roller moving up the cove.

"Actually," he went on, "there's nothing wrong with what Jones did, except that it just isn't done. If the cops had gathered anything as open and shut as Jones was making this out to be, they wouldn't have tipped their mitts. They'd never have given Jones all that information. They'd have saved it to bring out at the trial. A defense attorney couldn't ask for anything better than to have the coroner map the prosecution's case. So it's pretty much a cinch the cops didn't put Jones up to this, or give him that dope on Dawson."

"He could have found it out himself," she suggested.

"He could have. And he could have invented the atom bomb, too, but he didn't. Jones is no ball of fire. He didn't dig up that dirt about Bull's girl down in Portland, not in two days. How would he go about finding that out? The only way anybody would know what Dawson did at the convention in Portland is to have followed him, and the only people who would care enough to have him shadowed would be his enemies. That could be the lumber people, probably Gentry, or somebody in a rival union. My bet is Gentry, because union people would have a hard time talking Jones into giving Dawson the works. Gentry would have no trouble at all. He's got a million reasons, all in the bank."

He had said it, all the way through, start to finish, and it sounded as right in words as when it was an unspoken conviction. But he had not finished, not quite. He had not asked her the question, *What were you doing at Dawson's?* And he had not asked himself, *What are you going to do about it?*

"But if you do not think Dawson killed her, who. . ."

"I wish I knew." He looked straight at her. "You didn't, did you?"

She smiled a small, formal, uncertain smile. "No, I did not kill her."

"I didn't think you did," he said quickly, making it sound almost as though his question had been a joke. "But why did you run?"

"I was afraid. I had no business there. I thought you were a policeman."

"What were you doing there?"

She did not look at him as she answered. She stared out through the breath-fogged window at the ocean, but her words were direct. "I was coming home from the Berrys— Ruth and Joe. Joe works until one o'clock, and Ruth is in the hospital having another baby. I've been looking after their children until Joe gets home at night. I was walking home from there when I saw people standing in front of the Dawsons' place. Mr. Lazarevich was there and he told me what had happened. So I went in."

"The front door?"

"No, the back door. I went around down the alley and I looked in the window first and there wasn't anybody there, so I went in. You came and I was afraid, so I ran away."

"What about when I came to your place yesterday?"

"I thought you were a policeman and I was afraid."

"That's a hell of a way to act with a policeman."

"I know."

"If I'd been a policeman you'd have been in a mess."

"I thought of that later."

"But when I said hello at the city hall, you still weren't talking."

"I was upset. About the inquest. You startled me."

"For a girl who breaks into houses to look at corpses, you startle easy."

For a moment he thought she was going to cry. But she didn't. She began to talk, not about what they had been talking about—her presence in the house—but about why it was she frightened easily. For she did. Many things frightened her. She did not know why she told him; probably it was because she did not want to say why she had gone to see the room Dee Dawson died in, but it might have been—at least partly—because he could say hello in Croatian and would trade the Cove city hall for Diocletian's palace in Split, Yugoslavia.

It had started ten years before, this matter of being afraid. She was fourteen years old then, a freshman in Cove High, a 10-B, for there was a junior high school. In Junior High she had been a fair student, and popular, although her clothes were not very good. There was little money in the family. Once there had been money, but her father, Felix, had spent it all, plus a great deal he did not have, on a trawler. The boat was purchased in 1929 and, for the next three seasons, fishing was not bad but selling was no good at all. And then they had no boat and no money either.

Felix Barovich did not believe in relief: a man who did not work should not receive money for not working. But there was no work. The family grew vegetables in the back yard, caught fish off the dock, dug goeducks on the beach, but they could not raise or catch or dig enough to feed a family of four. Besides there were bills—bills for school supplies, bills for lights, bills for clothes. So Felix Barovich took his relief check and felt ashamed, and the family felt his shame.

They were on relief a long time. Then there were the big strikes. Strikes everywhere. At the mill, in the woods, on the docks. And for Felix Barovich, strikes meant jobs that paid good money; the men who went to work while the strike was on got more money than the men who were on strike. You got a bonus to make up for the friends you lost crossing picket lines, and for the danger. But for Felix Barovich, self-respect was measured in dollars and cents. He was not a union man. A picket line was just a bunch of men who swore at you, called you names, and, if they got a chance, beat hell out of you. Felix Barovich was not afraid of being beaten up, and even less was he afraid of being called names. But his daughter was.

It is not good when you are a freshman to have your chums stop speaking to you. It is awful. And it is worse if the misfortune of being different because your father is a strike breaker is added to that of being different because your folks talk Croatian at home and do not sound like other girls' folks when they use English.

The waterfront strike started during her freshman year. It lasted longer than any of the other strikes. The kids of the strikers got hungrier, and meaner. Monica began to find notes in her books, notes in which was written only one word, a word ugly and crawly as a spider crab, the word *Scab*.

The Tuesday before Thanksgiving there was a riot on the waterfront. Two men were killed, a policeman and a striker. The next day at school somebody slipped a note in her history book during the pep rally in the assembly hall; she found it after she was home:

> Crow, crow,
> Why don't you go?
> You aren't wanted here.
>
> Scab, scab,
> We have a slab
> For you if you stay here.
>
> Fink, Fink,
> Gee, but you stink.
> You aren't wanted here.

Catlicker, catlicker,
Dirty old ratlicker,
You aren't wanted here.

That night somebody threw a rock through the kitchen
window, barely missing her mother and sprinkling glass in
the food on the stove. A few minutes later the doorbell rang.
Monica went to the door and was struck by flying garbage. A
rotting potato bloodied her nose.

On Thanksgiving Day her brother made an awful mistake
in the football game. The kids at school were as mean as if
he had done it on purpose. They seemed to think he *had*
done it on purpose. She could not understand how they felt.

The strike was settled before Christmas. Things were
better at school, though it was only a few months until the
family was back on relief. She had never been popular after
the strike. It was hard to make friends. She felt different.
People scared her. Did he understand?"

Yes, he understood. Seward understood more than she
had said. He had known a lot of immigrant kids who had
been crunched between the grindstones of two cultures; most
of them had turned their backs on the old and embraced
with passion the new. But here was one who walked alone,
differing from her parents, differing from the peasant girls
who came in gay skirts to the markets of Split on Sundays,
differing from the Slav girls who went dancing at the road-
houses on the Ocean Road each Saturday night.

But he did not understand what compulsion had driven
this girl to enter a stranger's house to look on a body. And,
feeling sorry for her, he could not ask. Could he say: Did you
think your brother had done it? He could not. A hell of a
reporter, he was.

He glanced at his watch: a quarter past five. They had
been gone more than two hours, and he was overdue at the
office. He eased the Olds out from between the picnic tables

and they drove back to town. The evening closed around them and darkness shut them ever more into a world of their own. They talked about Yugoslavia.

A mile from town the headlights picked up the figure of an old man in a worn plaid shirt and work pants. Seward breaked sharply to offer him a lift, but the tramp looked with blind fright into the glare of the lights, then plunged off the road and disappeared among the charred stumps.

Seward said, "Some of those old beach rats get crazy as coots, living alone."

Monica Barovich said something about canned heat and turned the conversation back to Croatia.

He slowed down as he passed Logger Hall. The lights from the windows reflected on the brown water of the Tala. They both looked up at the windows, but they kept the conversation away from Bull Dawson. He parked for a few minutes in front of her house, the engine of the Olds idling smoothly, while she finished telling him about her uncle, who was still in Yugoslavia. When she finished her account, he said, meaning it, "I've got to get back to the office now. I'm really glad to have met you, Miss Barovich. I hope we can get together again."

"I'm afraid I must have bored you, Mr. Seward. I'm not much of a talker usually. I don't know what got into me."

"I enjoyed every minute of it. I intend to hear a lot more," he said. "It seems. . ." Remembering what he most wanted to hear her talk about, he stopped. The pause lengthened into embarrassment, but he could think of no way to end the sentence.

Monica Barovich opened the car door with her elbow and said, "There is one thing I must tell you, Gale. You would find it out anyway, if I did not tell you. That is, if you wanted to find out."

He waited, almost afraid to hear it.

"I wasn't really born in Split. I only wish I had been." And having made the confession, which was a confession only by her standards, she pushed open the door and ran through the rain up the wooden steps of the front porch. At the door she turned, waved, and disappeared inside.

He drove back to the office, dissatisfied with himself and the world.

The ad manager did not mind Gale's tardy return with the Olds; he was still working on the next day's layout, trying to put each ad in a position where the merchant who had purchased it would be happy—an ad manager's daily battle with impossibility. He barely looked up when Seward returned the car keys.

Joe Kalinen had left his story of the inquest on Seward's desk, along with a note that said he was out having dinner and meant he was out drinking beer. Seward started to edit the copy. "Union officials rioted yesterday afternoon at the coroner's inquest on the death of Delight Dawson after evidence was introduced that William 'Bull' Dawson was guilty of adultery."

Seward muttered, "Oh, for Christ sake." He rolled paper into his typewriter and began the job of rewriting. He was careful to qualify each statement ("according to Coroner Xenophon Jones"), to distinguish fact from imputation ("Jones implied without introducing evidence that Dawson had a two-day affair with a Portland girl") and to phone all the principals for statements. He wrote fast and well. The story had pace; the phrasing was good but not so flashy that it detracted from the information. But when he read the story over, marking in the subheads and the boldface, he recognized it for what it was: an impartial listing of the results of a partial inquisition.

He was deeply troubled.

— IX —

COUNTERPOINT

ARNE TOIVENEN had no doubts. He worked with the concentration and assurance of a man whose actions were in harmony with a long-felt, completely absorbed philosophy. To Toivenen, all life was struggle, class struggle, and the attempt to frame Bull Dawson neither shocked nor surprised him: It was what he had expected. He wasted no energy in resentment. He accepted the inquest for what it was, a challenge to battle, and even before he left the city hall he was planning the union counter-offensive.

The field was clear. Usually Toivenen had to argue, cajole and eventually compromise with Dawson, Plotch and Winter. But today Dawson was dazed with grief and alcohol; Plotch was still in jail; and Winter, though obviously in glum opposition to Toivenen's activities, could think of no adequate objections.

Toivenen asked Al Addison to take Dawson out for a shave, haircut and steam bath. This served the double purpose of making the martyr more presentable to the public and of keeping Addison from bailing Plotch out for a couple of hours. Although he liked Plotch, Toivenen did not feel like arguing strategy and tactics with him. At a time like this, one head was better than two.

The campaign Toivenen planned was obvious and uncomplicated. Its first objective was to put horns on Jones and Gentry; halos on Dawson and Plotch. If this did not force them to drop the attempt to frame Dawson, and he was sure it wouldn't, there would be a mass demonstration of protest.

129

Perhaps on something as raw as this, the other unions would cooperate in a general strike.

The local's high command assembled in the second floor offices of Logger Hall shortly after six P.M. Dawson was sober: the alcohol had been sweated out of his system by the steam bath, but his grief-fogged mind did not match his glowing skin. Plotch, out on fifty dollars bail, was let down after the emotional release of his inquest speech. Winter was glum, depressed by the bad publicity and the thought of what the struggle might do to the local's bank balance. Al Addison, as an outsider, was alert and interested. But Toivenen dominated the meeting, recommending tactics, explaining what he had already done, what the opposition would probably do.

He had tended to the details. The office mimeographs already were rolling out handbills. One asked, WHO BOUGHT JUDAS JONES?, and the other, "WHO IS JONES SHIELDING?" On the reverse sides were cartoons: one of Leo Plotch with the caption "Guilty—Of Believing in Justice"; the other, a locomotive with Jones's face on the boilerhead, was called "The Great Railroader."

It was decided the handbills would not be distributed until after the funeral.

The funeral was to be a show of force and solidarity. Toivenen had a telephone committee working on the membership, telling them to attend, rain or more rain. The other unions were being asked to cooperate.

Men had been assigned to watch Gentry's office and house, and Jones's house and funeral establishment, and to report on who came and went at each place.

Toivenen telephoned national headquarters and reported on developments. They were unexcited, but they promised to send a lawyer to work with Addison when the inquest was resumed.

"What about it, Al?" Toivenen asked the lawyer. "Just where *do* we stand legally? Can they get away with anything as bald as this?"

Addison ran his hand over his short, silvery hair, then studied the end of his cigar. Even outside the courtroom he used the attention-getting tricks of his trade. When everyone was watching, he began:

"The institution of the county coroner has outlived its purpose. Like the human tonsil, it is at best a useless appendage and at worst a source of poison to the rest of the system." He flicked the ash off the cigar, looked at Toivenen, and went on, "Nevertheless, it exists, and it is too late for surgery in this case.

"The status of a coroner's inquest is uncertain, legally. It isn't even known, for example, whether testimony given at an inquest is privileged, that is, whether it can be quoted without fear of libel. My personal opinion is that it would be difficult to win a libel suit based on testimony given at an inquest.

"The coroner is given the widest latitude in conducting an inquest. Since it is really not a court at all, the usual legal safeguards do not apply. I do not believe that Jones can deny Dawson the right of counsel, but I am sure he will be able to deny us the right to cross-examine witnesses."

Plotch asked, "What is the worst he can do?"

"Legally, the worst that could happen would be for the jury to say Bull killed her. Then the prosecuting attorney would get an information against him and the case would come to trial." He glanced at Dawson. "I assume that such a case could not be made to stick in court where the defense has a fair break. And it is quite likely that Jones isn't trying for an indictment. I think what he wants is to hang Bull's dirty linen on the line. Smear stuff. And it will be hard to prevent that."

"You mean Jones has us by the knockers."

Addison contemplated his cigar again. "I wouldn't phrase it quite that way, but the situation you describe approximates our legal position as far as the inquest is concerned. In court, it would be different."

Toivenen said, "But, Jesus, if we wait until we get into a real court, it's too damn late. You get an idea like that in peoples' heads and nothing will take it out. They believe what they hear first." He went to the window and looked across the river at the lights in the house on top of the hill. They seemed very high and far away. "But, by God, we can make this backfire. We'll tie up this town like a mummy. We'll give them a strike that *is* a strike." He turned to Plotch. "Look, Leo, will you go and see the Teamster guys and sound them out whether they'll go along with us. If we get them, the rest will fall in. We can count on the longshore guys. If we can shut down the camps, the waterfront and the trucks, the mills will goddam well go down, whether they strike or not. By God, they asked for it, and they're going to get it."

Plotch said, "I'll see what I can do. But whatever they decide, they'll have to clear with Seattle, and they're conservative as hell up there."

"No, wait." Dawson got out of his chair. Neatly dressed, shaved, with his hair combed, he still gave the impression of extreme fatigue, as though the faintest bump might cause him to collapse. He looked at each man before he spoke and his words came slowly. "Look, fellows, I didn't kill Dee and I can prove it. There's no use hauling the guys out on a strike for this. I'm not even sure we can get them out. It would be wildcat as hell. Jesus, a strike's no fun. I remember one when we had nothing to eat but soup and beans the last week. Dee never liked them either after that. I didn't kill her and I can prove it, and there's no use calling the guys out over this."

They all sat listening to the rain.

Addison said, "And you'd be breaking your contract."

Toivenen was on his feet again. He thrust his big bony face close to Dawson's thin face. "Dammit, Bull, you keep looking on this personally. This isn't anything personal. They aren't attacking you because you're a brown-haired guy with a thousand dollars in the bank and a house half paid for. They're after you because you're the most effective damn leader of a fighting union around here. What happens to Bull Dawson doesn't make a goddam bit of difference to anybody but the census taker and your next of kin, but what happens to the president of this local makes one hell of a difference. They know that, or they wouldn't be pulling this business. Christ, man, we don't even know that they didn't kill Dee just to frame you. And if you don't recognize it, it's just too bad, because the rest of us haven't any choice but fighting back. If we sit on our asses and wait until the legal processes are observed, we'll be screwed, blewed and tattooed. We got to hit back."

He swung around on Addison. "As for the contract, Gentry can stuff that until it sticks out his ears. We'll go into continuous session or some damn thing. Murders and frame-ups aren't covered by contracts."

Dawson sighed hugely. God Almighty, why did everything have to happen at once? "Okay. Handle it your way. Of course, you got to clear it with the men."

Plotch said, "I'll go over and see the Teamsters." He asked Addison, "What'll I tell them when they ask how I stand on my own troubles?"

"You'll probably get ten days."

Plotch smiled. "Well, they've built a better jail since the

last time I made it. Back in the Wobbly days it was a hell of a firetrap. Scare a man to death. And the cops are better behaved now. That Elliott is even a college boy." He put on his raincoat and went out with a "see you later."

With Plotch gone, Toivenen began pacing the room again. He was worried about the funeral. He wished there were some sure way to make it good propaganda. But he was afraid to ask Bull about that: the guy was already too close to the breaking point. He glanced at Dawson.

Dawson was staring at the rain-streaked window. "Christ," he said at last, "I hope it doesn't come to a strike. It's a bitch of a weather for a strike."

It was uncomfortable weather, too, for the men assigned by Toivenen to watch Jones and Gentry, though the rain combined with darkness to make their own discovery unlikely.

The man watching Gentry's office at the plywood plant sat under an empty boxcar and stared up at the darkened windows of the office; no one came near him and he saw nothing. The rain kept him from getting sleepy, but after midnight, convinced there was nothing to see, he went home.

The man assigned to Jones found shelter under a cherry tree that leaked. He was uncomfortable but, as he told himself, no more so than when hunting ducks. Through the window, he watched Jones eat a heavy dinner, answer the telephone, and shortly after seven o'clock leave the house and drive away in his plymouth coupé. Jones was back within an hour, and stayed home the rest of the evening.

Gentry's house on the hill was the worst spot. The venetian blinds were slanted shut on all windows except those fronting the cliff, and the man covering the house could not see in. Nor was there much shelter. After prowling uncomfortably around the grounds, the man bored into the shrubbery and lay on the loose wet earth about six feet from the front door.

As he waited, he wished he knew what was going on inside the house. He wished even harder that he was dry. And most of all, that he had remembered to bring a bottle.

The watching was good. To the house came, one at a time, the coroner, the chief of police and Rutherford Olson. Jones entered smiling, and stumped away angrily; Snow seemed worried as he stood under the porch light waiting to be admitted, and just as worried when he came out; Olson looked self-satisfied coming and going—he was talking to himself both ways, but the watcher could not catch the words.

Xenophon Jones was bewildered at his reception. When Gentry telephoned to say he wanted to see Jones at once, the coroner expected praise for his afternoon's performance; he responded to the summons with smiling alacrity. Entering Gentry's presence as an equal and coworker, he was amazed and abashed when treated as a bungling subordinate.

"But," he objected, when Gentry concluded his diatribe by calling the inquest an abysmal botch, "I felt things went well. I maneuvered him into a very precarious position, didn't I?"

Gentry tightened his lips across his teeth and shook his head. "I'll go over it again," he said with the patronizing patience of a teacher explaining simple arithmetic to the dullest pupil. "You were supposed to do it subtly. You know, subtly—not like an elephant coming down stairs. You were supposed to get Dawson involved in contradictions that would discredit his credibility. But you were supposed to act in sorrow rather than in anger. We don't care about getting an indictment. What we want is for all his people to know he was two-timing his wife. My God, you acted like you had him on trial for belonging to a union."

Jones was upset. Though he was not often invited to their homes, he felt himself a part of the governing class and he was sure the governing class did not like unions either. He said, "I thought you would want the union discredited."

"Oh, my God." Gentry refilled his own glass without offering Jones another drink. "Look. You ought to be able to see this. The last thing in the world you should do was give the impression you were sore at the union. You love that union, we love that union, every right-thinking God-fearing American loves that union from breakfast to bedtime. We love it very much and it grieves the hell out of us that a man like Dawson, honored and trusted by hundreds of good, self-respecting union men should err so grievously as to commit adultery and, perhaps, bash his wife's brains out with a blunt instrument. Do you follow me?"

"No." Jones morosely turned the empty glass in his hand; he was determined not to understand anything as long as he was unappreciated.

Gentry realized he was making his man balky. He poured Jones another drink, but he was so angry his hand shook and he sloshed whiskey on the floor.

"Look," Gentry began again, "If we push Dawson around on the ground that he is a union leader, some people may get the idea we're not impartial. See? They may think we are trying to discredit him because he is a union officer, not because he slugged his wife. They may leap to all sorts of wrong conclusions. All we want to do is discredit him, not the union. Everybody knows he's president of the local without your underlining it, for Christ sake. Now when you get back in there tomorrow—"

"The day after tomorrow," interrupted Jones, who had noticed the lapse from *we* to *you* in Gentry's speech. "Tomorrow is the funeral."

"Day after tomorrow then. But remember not to mention the union. Be solicitous. Let him have counsel. Help him to establish an alibi—we can break it down later—but take it easy on him when asking questions. Be gentle. Wrap him up in cotton. You can't undo what you did today, but you can make it look like you had a hangover or a bellyache. Okay?"

And Jones, who might have understood Gentry if understanding had not meant giving up the pleasant conviction that he had been brilliant at the inquest, looked at the man who represented everything Jones thought himself entitled to—power, respect, wealth—and said, "Yes, it's all right. I'll treat him gently."

He felt better when Gentry said, "Good, I knew we could count on you, once you understood. I'm sorry we didn't make it clear earlier."

The fine whiskey mellowed Jones further. But when Gentry, walking with him to the door, said, "Now remember, take it easy. No more histrionics," Jones was again hurt. He strode through the rain to his Plymouth, muttering to himself, "You were superb, you were superb, you were superb."

Gentry's interview with Snow was on a different basis. Their relationship to each other in the crisis had not been established; over their whiskeys in the leather-and-mahogany den they eyed each other speculatively, and for a time their conversation was polite and pointless. Finally Gentry asked, "What did you say to Jones just before the inquest ended?"

"You weren't there. How do you know I said anything?"

"I had people there."

"Did they tell you about Elliott?"

Gentry's look of surprise told Snow that he had not known.

"He wanted to testify," Snow explained.

Gentry poured another drink for the Chief but did not refill his own glass.

Snow said, "I gather that you know what Elliott knows."

After a considerable pause, Gentry said carefully, "I believe that he arrested Steve Barovich a few weeks ago."

"Exactly."

"And you released him."

Snow grinned a humorless grin. "So?"

"So perhaps we have a common interest in this."

"Perhaps."

"You think not?"

Snow turned on the grin again. "I like to be helpful, Gordon, and if I can do you a favor I'll be glad to. But I can't stick my neck out too far. Being Chief is how I make my living; and if I got bounced from this job I couldn't retire on my savings. I'd hate to have to go to work, so to speak. As long as things go smoothly, I'll let well enough alone. But if things get hot and somebody wants to know where Steve Barovich was between nine and eleven o'clock on the night Mrs. Dawson was killed, I'm damn well going to run him in. And if he can't give a pretty good story about where he was that night, he's had it as far as I'm concerned."

"Wouldn't that be inconvenient for you?"

"Not half as inconvenient as not running him in would be, if Elliott talks."

"Then Elliott better not talk."

"He will, though, sooner or later. He's bucking for my job and he figures he's got me where the hair is short."

"Then we do have something in common after all."

Snow shrugged. "Maybe so, Gordon, but the easiest way out for me is to run in Barovich, throw the hooks into him, and let him worry about wriggling off."

"I don't want that."

"I'd be sorry to do anything you didn't want. But the big I comes first."

"What if Barovich spoke of certain arrangements he has had with you?"

"That bastard sure can keep a secret, can't he?" Snow grinned again, this time meaning it. "Under the circumstances, nobody would believe him, do you think?"

"I suppose not. The best thing then is for Elliott to be kept quiet, if that can be arranged."

"That's how it looks from my seat in the bleachers. But it's easier said than done."

"Don't you have anything on him that would shut him up?"

"Not a damn thing."

Gentry walked about the room. It was a short walk, and at the end of it he found himself facing the trophy cabinet with its big action picture and the clipping in which Grantland Rice called him the coolest player under fire ever to appear in the Rose Bowl.

"How's Elliott fixed financially?"

"Not so hot. Unless he's got some graft I don't know about."

"Does he ever pick things up on the side?"

"Not that I know of. He's a very moral guy."

Gentry smiled into his faint reflection in the glass of the trophy case. From long experience he had learned that the purchase price of a moral man with a small bank balance was lower than that of an immoral man with money. He turned, poured Snow another drink, and this time filled his own glass. He lowered himself into a chair, and after appropriate attention to his drink he said, "The lumber game is a strange business, Chief."

"I'll bet."

"A man who keeps his eyes open can make a fortune, almost overnight."

"No kidding."

"I mean it. Overnight. For example, we're buying up some

timber from the state this week. Going to outbid everybody, regardless. But there's some land between our present holdings and the new stuff that we'll need when they work the new timber. I guess it's perfectly safe, but if some smart operator were to get in ahead of us and grab that strip, he'd practically be able to name his price."

Snow thought it over. "What sort of a profit could that hypothetical operator wring out of your bloodless corporation?"

"It's hard to say. Maybe ten thousand dollars."

"That's not a lot of money."

"It might be more. Maybe as much as twenty-five thousand."

"That's not bad for overnight."

"That's right. Overnight. It's a funny business, logging."

"Here's to it," said Snow.

They emptied their glasses.

It was what Snow had wanted, help from Gentry in silencing Elliott. But now that the offer was made, he was not happy. He held in his hands the power that would make Elliott well-to-do; and the thought of Elliott making twenty-five thousand dollars overnight, the vision of Elliott with money in the bank, the realization that Elliott would simply quit rather than pound a penitential beat, wrung Snow's stomach. He did not doubt that Elliott would take the bribe. It was too much money to turn down.

All the way back to the station he thought of how much money it was.

Gentry, who had matched drinks with two men, was feeling capable and powerful when Olson dropped in uninvited for a chat. He was glad to see the publisher, though usually he considered the old coot a bore. They had a drink. It was Olson who brought up the matter of the murder.

"The *Logger* hasn't taken an editorial position," he explained, "and I'm sounding out responsible opinion before unleashing my editorial drums."

"I'm glad you came to me, Senator. I appreciate the compliment. You know, I was just thinking before you came in that it is interesting how much responsible opinion has shifted. Why, a year ago the better element in the community would have welcomed the disgusting display poor old Jones made of himself this afternoon."

Olson said, "Yes, indeed," but his expression showed that he was puzzled.

Gentry talked on rapidly. "Yes, a year ago we might not have been able to see farther than the ends of our noses. But now, taking the long view—and I must say, Senator, that the *Logger* has played a vital role in civic education—now it is easy for us to see the danger in alienating labor. We must not be needlessly harsh. It is foolish to arouse labor's distrust in the normal processes of government. And that is what Jones was doing by his attack on Dawson as a union man. Not that I doubt for a moment that Bull killed her. Of course he did. But in a case like this, he should be brought to justice as a man, not as a labor leader. We must not make all union men think we regard them as murderers, simply because Dawson is one. You agree, I'm sure, Senator."

After a few more drinks Olson agreed fully.

Later that evening, when Olson dropped in at the *Logger,* he startled Seward by suggesting that he write an editorial criticizing Jones for bias in handling the inquest.

"I'll do it right away."

"No, make it tomorrow. It would be more effective on the morning the inquest is to resume." He breathed whiskey at his city editor and, on an impulse, patted him on the shoulder. "You have the makings of a fine newspaperman, my boy. Another few years and you'll have learned all the tricks of the trade. It's great experience for you." He got as far as the door, looked back, and repeated, "All the tricks of the trade."

Seward rubbed his hand across his face, sighed, and wondered vaguely who'd been pumping the Boss full of alcohol and subversive ideas.

— X –

NOCTURNE

LONG after the whine of the auto's wheel on the wet blacktop had died away, the old man came out from the field of stumps. He was wet and muddy and breathless. The rain had matted his gray hair, and there were small clots of dirt in his four-day beard. He walked miserably into town and lurched into the first tavern he saw.

It was an old beer parlor, a relic of the great days of logging on the cove—a place with sawdust on the floor, popcorn and pickled beets on the counter, a picture of the Frank Gotch-Scissors Joe Stecher match on the wall, and a barkeep with hair parted in the middle and plastered into a bang on his forehead.

The barkeep was accustomed to queer customers, and he knew by sight the old man who came in out of the rain and sat mumbling in a corner. He served the old man beer as long as his money lasted, then bribed him to leave with the gift of a bottle.

The old man knocked off the neck against a lamppost and drank the beer in three long swigs.

Then, his memory reaching through the haze that hung over his mind, he walked down to the river, followed it to the Old Bridge and, crawling under its shelter, went to sleep.

— XI —

THE FUNERAL

THE wind blew steadily from the southwest, a warm wet wind that cooled as it rose over the bold shore line and dropped its rain as it moved across the coastal mountains. It blew without gusts, a steady wind bringing a steady rain.

Back in the foothills the tops of the firs raked the bottoms of the gray cloud mass that pushed past, rotating eastward, and here too the rain fell, cascading down the drooping, shiny-needled branches and falling onto the needle mat that floored the forest. The carpeted earth soaked up the water, spongelike, but in time it was saturated and puddles formed in the dented tracks left by elk and deer, in the cavities torn by storm-felled trees, in the holes dug by squirrels and marmots. And in the logged-off lands where fires had swept the slash and skimmed the young vegetation, the water gathered in rivulets, the rivulets formed creeks, and the creeks rushed, brown and heavy, toward the Tala River. The rain that fell on a thousand square miles of coastal mountains oozed through the root-knit earth and raced through scarred stumpland to merge in the Tala. The river rose.

And the sea rose. The tide pulsed into the cove. A steady procession of wind-piled waves surged at the bar, sweeping in, long and ominous and dull gray, rushing from the nowhere of the horizon to break in a froth of green-white on the dirty side of the bar, rushing and smashing, lying calm inside the bar, and then being picked up again by the wind, charging down the five-mile length of the inlet against the wharfs and bulkheads, steadily, relentlessly beating against the wharfs and bulkheads.

Salt water pushed back through the pipes that had been laid to carry away the rain, and along Elm Street fountains of water geysered from the sewer vents. It had happened often before, and the street had high curbs to channel the water and let it run off into the river. But the merchants consulted the tide tables they received each year along with their calendars, and the tables showed that for the next two days the tides would be even higher. If it kept on raining, there would be a bad flood.

Rain softened the rawness of the lumber town. The unpainted shingle roofs darkened, and on each the faint froth of moss showed vividly green against the wet wood; lights glowed yellow and soft in the windows; the tangle of wires was lost against the gray of the sky and the dark of the streets. The town looked all of a piece, and there was a unity of thought centering about the rain, for the rain meant the same thing to everyone: discomfort and threat.

Even Ruth Peterson Gentry, looking down on the town from the cantilevered house atop the hill, worried as she watched the rising river. She could remember the big flood of 'thirty-three, when the Mill was shut for two weeks, the stores were swamped, and somebody had rowed into the lobby of the hotel for the benefit of the newsreel men. She wondered briefly if the cliff might be undermined by another such flood, but decided it wouldn't, and stood watching the workers gather at the chapel for Dee Dawson's funeral.

Because of the rain, few started for the chapel until the last minute. Then, all at once, the streets were crowded with people moving toward the undertaking establishment. The men wore slickers and old felt hats with the brims turned down; the women were in cheap raincoats or old tweed coats and they carried umbrellas to protect their Sunday hats. They walked fast through the rain, pausing only at the intersections on Elm Street to look for the best place to ford the flooded roadway. Many came in cars, old cars, even Model T's, and the cars of the workers lined the streets for blocks.

Everyone walked fast until near the chapel, then slowed self-consciously and with dignity mounted the cement steps and went through the double door into the presence of death. The seats were all taken. Men stood bareheaded and solemn in the aisles, along the wall at the back of the chapel, in the hallway. By the time the organ began to drone, latecomers were standing in the street. When they heard the music through the open door, they took off their hats and stood bareheaded in the rain.

At two-fifteen someone set off the old air-raid siren on the city hall, and at the sound of its wailing the men at the plywood plant and the mill stepped back from the positions, those who could do so without endangering themselves or the run, and stood in silence for five minutes.

The minister was young and he did not find the thought of death comfortable. When he came from the office into the chapel crowded with wet, intent, solemn people and, mounting the platform, saw through the open door the faces of hundreds more in the street, he was disturbed. There were more people than came to hear him on Easter, and he had prepared only a few words of condolence for the bereaved. He had to decide whether to pitch his voice for those in the street or to speak softly for the benefit of the relatives sitting in the privacy of the screened booth behind him.

The organ stopped with a sigh. The minister raised his voice. "Beloved, there is no death. . ."

In the screened booth four men sat on separate chairs and stared at separate spots of the dirty green carpet. Ano

Pelinen, the dead girl's father, a big, wistful man who was a fisherman and had known much sorrow, thought of nothing; he let sadness flow around him like a warm bath. Calvin Pelinen, her brother, kept wondering how the Red Sox were coming out with the A's, and from time to time felt guilty that he did not feel anything at all about losing his sister.

Bull Dawson tried to listen to the minister, but the voice was loud and hesitant and the words made no sense, for if there was no death there was something just as ugly and final and he had seen it. The words of praise meant nothing either, for they came from a man who had not known her well and who was praising Dee for qualities that were not Dee at all. After a time Bull heard the loud voice and did not hear the words, and he wished there was some place he could get a drink.

Arne Toivenen, who had come with Dawson to see that he did not get a drink, listened intently to the sermon, following not only the words but the mood of the minister. He was relieved when the young man, finding courage in the sound of his own sermon, lost his uneasiness. The voice took on timbre; the platitudes rolled like organ music, strong and familiar, right for the occasion, well-worn words as unobstrusive as old clothing, spoken with a religious emphasis that divorced them from reality.

Toivenen got up and looked again through a peephole in the screen into the faces of the crowd. The faces had a common expression; they had lost self-consciousness and the usual funeral look of polite sorrow. The expression was one of bewilderment and puzzled anger and determination; and even those who had come out of curiosity or to experience the guilty triumph of seeing the body of someone they had not liked, wore the expression. Toivenen thought, *This has got to them. They feel it. God, if I could just make it so they'd remember.*

The mood that rested on them was momentary: it grew out of their shared experiences and emotions—the funeral, the rain, the platitudes of the young man in the pulpit; in all probability it would not outlast the flowers on the coffin. Even among the union members, Toivenen knew, the sense of a common cause would not last; only a crisis could weld the men into a group capable of united action, and then but for a short time. The mood would pass. Inevitably the people would split: the conservatives would hate the liberals, the passive would distrust the militant; those without the power of office would lust after power, and the officers would think in terms of job-holding. Nothing Toivenen could do would stop this. But if, before the dissolution began, some dramatic incident occurred, the memory of their feeling of oneness might be driven deep into each individual. And, sitting in the chamber of the bereaved, Toivenen tried to think of some way to fulfill the dramatic possibilities of the funeral. He could not.

The preacher concluded his oration with a prayer; the organ moaned from the alcove; the solemn people filed past the coffin and peered in to fix in their memories an image of the girl as she never was. The pallbearers came and, surprised at its heaviness, carried the coffin to the hearse. They felt sad about the coffin getting wet, as though it might be spoiled.

The spectators hurried to their autos; the grind of starters and throb of motors sounded against the steady beat of the unhurried rain.

The family party came from the chapel, ducked their heads against rain and stares, hastened to the undertaker's sedan, a Packard with black flags on the fenders, that moved off at once behind the hearse. The other cars wheeled out from the curb and joined the slow procession.

Those who owned no cars and in the surge had met no

friends who offered rides stood on the wet sidewalks and watched the cars move past. They stood solemnly, looking at the familiar old Fords and Chevs and Plymouths bearing their neighbors and acquaintances, and the procession seemed impressive and beautiful and somehow important.

The last car passed. The spectators stood looking after it. Then, suddenly, without plan, the thing happened.

A half-dozen men standing together on the corner stepped out into the street and fell in behind the procession. They walked abreast. And Toivenen, who had waited in the crowd, trying vainly to think of a gesture just this simple and natural, fell in behind the leaders. Others followed until three hundred men and women were marching silently, out of step, impressive, along the flooded streets, past the false-fronted stores and the solid old houses set on the high bank, over the bridge, and out to the green, granite-studded ground where Delight Pelinen was to be buried.

From the doorways of the shops and the windows of the houses the citizens of Cove watched the procession pass.

During the first half of the march, Toivenen was trapped in his emotions. He moved unthinkingly with the crowd, his head unbowed; he felt rather than thought, and his emotions told him this was good. When the procession passed unhesitatingly under the red stoplight at the main intersection and he looked at the line of cars held up by the marchers, he was aroused from his reverie: but his mind, too, told him this was good. He wondered if there was some way to make it better. He considered singing, but decided singing would be bad. They marched on in silence until they reached the cemetery.

A canopy stood over the grave. The rain slanted in beneath the canopy and splashed into the muddy pool at the bottom. The flowers banked around the grave were heavy with water but their colors were vibrant. There were many flowers, and there were many people. They stood well back from the grave, not crowding, for the grave had the threat of a chasm; and when the minister came they parted silently to let him through. Soon after they parted again for the dead girl's husband and father and brother.

Toivenen worked his way through to the inner edge of the crowd. The tableau seemed to lack drama, though the floral offerings banked beside the grave pleased him. The largest wreath was in the shape of a harp. It stood on the far side of the grave from him, but even at a distance he could read the card on which a florist had printed, "Herman Peterson and Family."

This time Toivenen knew exactly what to do. Slowly, respectfully, but in full view of the crowd, he walked around the grave, picked up the flowers that Old Herm had ordered for the man who had lost his wife, and carried them away, through the ranks of the people, who stepped back as he approached, then closed behind him.

It was the gesture he had wanted: a repudiation of friendly relations, an acceptance of the challenge of the inquest.

Behind him, Bull Dawson stood with bowed head, staring at the muddy ground, his mind blank.

The young minister self-consciously spread his arms. In a few minutes it was over.

Dawson rode back from the funeral in the car with the minister. He felt better than he had since Dee's death. In the ceremony at the graveside he had been warmed by the eternal hope of the phrases about resurrection; the divorcing finality of the dirt falling on the coffin had filled him with the dignity of tragedy. He had not noticed Toivenen's disposal of the flowers; the funeral, which Toivenen had dramatized as a symbol of working-class unity, left Dawson feeling alone, but strong in his loneliness.

He was grateful to the minister. On the drive back to the chapel he stole glances at the boyish face above the reversed collar. He wondered how a man so young could be so wise. Were all ministers that smart? He tried to remember Dr. Bailey, who was pastor of the church his mother had taken him to, but he could recall nothing except the hardness of the seats, Bailey's beard, and Bailey's habit of saying *Now in conclusion* at least five times in each sermon. Maybe ministers were smarter nowadays.

The car drew up in front of the chapel. The young man put his hand on Dawson's shoulder, squeezed firmly, and said, "We must accept the will of the Lord."

Dawson did not want him to leave. He wanted more of the strength he had drawn from the young man. "Reverend, could I talk to you a little?"

A shadow crossed the minister's face. It had been a moving funeral, a very moving funeral, and he was anxious to get home and tell his wife about it. The congregation was the largest he had addressed since he was called to Cove, and he knew he had impressed them. Something like this could be the turning point of his ministry; they might get a call to some more fashionable church in a town where it did not always rain. He wanted very much to get home and talk about it. But he leaned back in the seat and said, "Certainly, Mr. Dawson. What is it?"

The driver, a boy who worked for the undertaker, got out of the front seat and left them alone.

Dawson fumbled for something to say. "About the offering, Reverend . . ."

The minister was still embarrassed at the thought of receiving a fee for a funeral; making money out of death seemed in some obscure way to be tempting fate. He looked away and said, "That is taken care of through the parlors, Mr. Dawson."

"Oh."

The silence grew between them. They listened to the rain drum on the metal roof of the Packard and each waited for the other to speak. Finally the minister asked, "Was there anything else?"

The feeling of strength was fading fast, and Bull Dawson wanted very much to recapture it. He wanted to hear again the great certainties that had so moved him at the graveside. He tried to frame a question, but all he could ask was, "Why?"

The minister tried to answer. He talked of acceptance, of courage in the face of adversity, of how Mrs. Dawson would have wanted her husband to behave in this time of trial. He talked for a long time, but Dawson did not follow his words for long, no longer than it took him to realize the boy was talking nonsense. Dawson's thoughts were on his life with Dee. He had been jealous, suspicious; there had been talk about her, and he had believed some of it—still did, for that matter, though it seemed unimportant now; they had fought, and they had always, sooner or later, made up. He wondered how many others there had been.

"I suggest," the young man was saying, "that you become interested in some activity important to mankind. If you cannot live to love, you can live to serve."

Dawson thought of the union and of the work there was to do; he did not feel much like doing it. He remembered the inquest and his anger rose: there was one thing he'd like to do—get Jones in a dark alley.

The minister was still talking, carried away again by the sound of his own voice. ". . . it might be church work, Mr. Dawson. If you care to interest yourself in church work, there is always room in our congregation for another soul. There is always room in Christ for . . ."

"Thank you, Reverend," Dawson said. He could not even remember the minister's name, or what denomination he represented. "You have been a big help. I appreciate it."

He fumbled for the door handle, found it, and stepped into the flooded street.

The minister looked after him, his mouth open above the reversed collar.

Bull Dawson walked slowly across the street and around the corner. Then he broke into a run. He ran all the way to the speakeasy.

— XII —

STEVE

MONICA BAROVICH stared across the sink and out the rain-streaked window. The paint on the house next door was bubbled and broken; there was a V-shaped rip in the pulled window shade and a crack in the glass. She wished the Koskis would paint the house and get a new blind. And more glass. That window always reminded her of a day at a school picnic —the Junior Class picnic—when she'd found one of the boys interested in her. They'd talked about things, and he told her about breaking a window with a football, and she told him of the time, back in the old country, when her mother had broken a window in their house and had—but he had interrupted, "You mean they have glass in the windows, like white people?" She had tried not to show that she was hurt.

She wondered what Gale Seward would say about that story. Could she tell him about it the next time she saw him? It had been a long time since she had been able to talk to anyone about Yugoslavia. Her mother could tell her about cooking and courtship and sewing—little more; her brother wasn't interested.

She ran more water into the sink and swirled up the suds. Seward was interested, though. He knew a lot about the country. She looked again out the window at the slanting rain, and hummed a snatch of "Kisa Pada," the part that told of the good crops that would follow the rain.

Steve came in, unshaved, his dark hair tousled. He was whistling "You Are My Sunshine." Monica stopped humming

154

and glanced at the clock on top of the stove—eleven-thirty. "You are up early."

"Okay, I'm a sack rat."

"I was not complaining. I was remarking."

"Sure, you're a remarkable girl. Woman, that is."

He washed his hands in the kitchen sink, doused his hair and combed it; the water flipped off his comb and popped and sputtered on the glowing top of the range. She told him the bathroom was upstairs and he told her he knew it but that he was downstairs. It went like that until lunch was ready. It so often went like that. She wished it didn't go like that, because a family is all one has, even a family composed of a morose brother and a sad, broken mother who stares all day at nothing. But it was like that more and more.

They ate lunch almost in silence. Her mother asked for things in Croatian and her brother replied in English. Monica said *molim* and *hvala* to her mother, and *please* and *thank you* to her brother.

Steve Barovich left the table before the others finished and took his raincoat from the cupboard housing the hot-water tank.

"Are you going out?" Monica asked.

"No, I'm putting this on to wear in the living room."

"Are you going to the funeral?"

He looked her in the eye. "Is there any reason why I should?"

"Is there any reason why you should not?"

He glared across the room. "So that's what you think. Well, you're wrong." He turned abruptly and went out, slamming the kitchen door behind him.

"*Sta je ovo?*"

"It is nothing, mother. I thought he should go to the funeral of a friend's wife, as a matter of courtesy."

It was easy to lie to her mother, so easy to protect her from trouble she might not even recognize as trouble. Her mother did not even think it strange that Steven had so much money when he seldom went to work.

The question of Steve's money had troubled Monica for a long time, until one night her brother had come in stumbling drunk and she had put him to bed; when unexpectedly he thanked her, she begged him to stay out of trouble. "Don' worry, baby, I can take care myself. Friend o' the Chief's." and he had told her a little of what he was doing.

She said it was wrong.

He laughed and said, "Look what those bastards did to me," and he was asleep.

The next day when she tried to talk to him about it, he told her to button her goddam lip and forget it. She could be quiet, but she could not forget.

It twisted her inside to think about it now. She was ashamed that the first thing she had thought when she heard of Dee Dawson's death was that Steve might have killed her. A sister should not think that about her only brother. Somehow, it had seemed that night that if she looked at the dead girl she would know if Steve had done it. She had gone to the kitchen: the body had been taken away, but she looked around the room. It had not helped. She still did not know.

While she washed the lunch dishes she looked at the grayness of the rain. She did not sing again. Her stomach was clamped in a tight knot, as was her mind.

After leaving the kitchen, Steve Barovich walked aimlessly through the rain. He liked rain. He crossed the bridge, waded Elm Street and went down to the beach. The tide was high, but receding; as each curling wave fell back it rolled the pebbles and the beach growled. A lone gull skidded across the face of the wind.

He watched the bird. If he had a gun, he could kill it.

Even with a twenty-two. He raised the imaginary gun, sighted quickly, squeezed off the shot. Then he was telling the sports writers who asked him how it felt to be the world's best shot that it was just luck, he wasn't that good, but they knew he was and so did he.

Barovich walked on, his feet careless of the beach muck, a vague smile on his face. He was dreaming out a familiar fantasy:

It was the second half of the Thanksgiving Day game, and this time Cove was behind by a point. There were seconds to play. Cove had the ball deep in its own territory. He studied the Sawton defense. They were playing back, expecting a desperation pass. He called for a quarterback sneak, a play designed only to gain a yard or two. The captain yelled signals over. He repeated it, 17-A, quarterback sneak. There was no time to argue. The play stood. They came out of the huddle. The backfield shifted and the sod felt good under his feet. He chanted the signals. The ball spiraled back into his hands and he spun quickly to his left, faked to the halfback who raced by and then, head down, he charged forward over the guard spot. The hole was open. He burst through the first line of defense. The defensive full crossed over at him and he slammed the heel of his free hand into the tackler's neck, knocking him off balance. For a moment he hesitated, surveying the field, then he was off, charging right over the defensive halfback, plunging on, watching the two safety men converge on him, timing it, timing it, turning on the speed at the last possible second, slipping between them (their pads creaked as they smacked into each other behind him and he heard them grunt) and he sprinted on, alone, sprinting straight to the touchdown, the winning touchdown. The headlines read: STEVE BAROVICH SAVES GAME. They were front-page headlines and everybody said it was too bad he was too modest to keep a scrapbook.

He picked up a flat rock and threw it underhand at the water, trying to skip it, but it hit a wave and disappeared. He tried again, but without luck. And, failing, he knew he had failed before. He could not kid himself. He had not saved the Thanksgiving game, he had lost it, lost it with his backward run, and there'd never been another Sawton game for him.

Bitchmonkey. They could of stopped me. One of our guys could have stopped me. They didn't because the old man was on strike. Dirty bastards.

The rain was coming harder. He walked on a little farther, but there was no joy in it and he turned back. Before he reached town he had a destination. He went straight to Snug Harbor.

For three dollars he could always conquer Irish.

— XIII —

NELLIE

Less than a cupful of coffee was left in the Silex when Nellie came into the kitchen after a poor morning's sleep. She drank it black. It was bitter and tasted reboiled, no help at all. She started to make more, but the coffee tin was empty.

"Hey, Irish, where the hell's the coffee?"

Irish's voice came from the bathroom. "We're fresh out."

"Why didn't you go and get more? Whoever kills it is supposed to get more right away."

"It's raining."

"You won't melt."

"Coffee isn't good for your blood pressure, anyway. You aren't as resilient as you used to be. You should lead a quiet life."

"Go to hell."

Irish came from the bathroom, her robe open. She had a good figure, better than Nellie's. "I'll go out and get it as soon as I get dressed, dear. Can't have you catching cold at your age."

Nellie knew Irish enjoyed making her angry. She tried to keep her temper, but she was too keyed up from lack of sleep and worry about her breast, which, whenever she thought of it, seemed to pain her. She said, "If I were running this place, you'd be out on the street fast."

"And if your grandmother had balls she'd be your grandfather."

Irish went into her room. Nellie put on a coat, a transparent slicker that reminded her of a contraceptive, took the purse with the grocery money from its hook in the cupboard and went out. She met Steve Barovich on the stairs.

"Hi, champ. You know enough to come in out of the rain."

"Sure thing. Irish in?"

"You bet."

"Thanks." He went on up. She knew Barovich on sight but couldn't remember anything about him, not even if she had ever had him or if he always took Irish. Irish had more regulars than she did. Goddam Irish, why did she have to harp so much on age? She felt old enough without Irish bringing it up every ten minutes. And this damned rain. She'd never get used to it. It was worse than the fog in Frisco or the cold in Fairbanks. Christ, but it could get cold at Fairbanks.

Elm Street was blocked by a line of cars, almost bumper to bumper. A funeral or something. She looked up the line and saw the hearse. The street was flooded, too, and she didn't feel like ducking between cars with water damn near up to her knees. That Irish!

She walked along the street for a block, looking for a good place to cross. Ah, the hell with it. She could buy the coffee later. It was too wet to stand around on street corners waiting to get across to the Safeway store. And too cold. Her breasts ached. She'd have to see a doctor. But what if it was cancer? Jesus, they might have to take off a breast. Wouldn't that please Irish? Irish could make some wonderful jokes out of that. Oh yes, she'd be funny as all hell about the potentialities of a one-breasted whore.

Nellie went into the Goal Line and asked for a coffee and hot butterhorn.

The Swede behind the counter said there were no butterhorns.

Doughnuts then.

He went for them.

She knew the Swede. He came around regularly but he never spoke to her outside the house, and she made it a point never to speak first on the street. Professional courtesy. Just plain common sense, for that matter. She ate the doughnuts, drank the coffee, and went out, feeling warmer and more melancholy.

The funeral procession had passed. She bogged across the street and bought a two-pound tin of coffee in the chain grocery. She saved the slip from the cash register; coffee cost two cents less at that store and Mrs. Dothan was always particular about keeping track of household expenses.

Nellie didn't feel like going back to the house. She hated the rain, but she hated the house more. She walked through the rain, walking fast, as though she were going somewhere, and afterward she could not remember the path that had brought her to the Old Bridge.

The bridge was ugly: a wooden drive set on a steel framework. It was built to swing sideways in the river when a boat needed to pass, and in the middle of the bridge a small house for the bridgetender straddled the roadway. It was dry under the house and the supporting girders broke the wind. Nellie stopped there and watched the river churn past.

The water was higher than she could remember having seen it, and browner, a rich earthy brown. There were lots of branches and bits of bark in the river. She would pick out a piece of wood when it was well upstream and watch it until it was out of sight on the other side of the bridge. She recalled a picnic she had gone to when she was a little girl; it was beside a waterfall, a little waterfall about five feet high, in a creek not far from the farm. Her folks were there; her brother too. She hadn't heard from her brother in years, not since her mother died; he had been in the Navy then. She wondered if he had been in the war—must have been; maybe he was at Pearl Harbor. He might be dead. She remembered the funeral procession on Elm Street, the long line of cars stretching out behind the hearse. If this was cancer and she died, who would go to her funeral? None of her customers, that was for damn sure. Mrs. Dothan. And Irish. Irish'd be glad to go. She'd probably be there hustling, that bitch.

Staring at the flowing water, thinking of Irish, she did not hear the man coming. She did not have the faintest idea anyone was near until he grabbed the purse. Then she was so surprised she just stood and watched him until he was half-way down the bridge. She ran after him then, but it was too late. He got off the bridge, ran into an alley, and she lost him.

Nellie leaned against a garage door and started to cry. Mrs. Dothan was going to be awfully sore. A man came up to her, and she turned on him fiercely, but he was a fat old man, very friendly, the bridgetender, and he said he had seen her running after the purse snatcher and had she got her purse back? She told him she hadn't, and he said she should report it to the police right away.

She couldn't think of any way to tell him she didn't want to go to the police. It wasn't that the cops treated her badly, but she just didn't like their attitude.

She said she didn't want to go to the trouble, and he said she ought to, that it was the plain duty of any citizen to report something like that. He walked with her as far as the city hall.

She was relieved when a boat whistle sounded and he had to run back to open the bridge.

He had been very nice and she felt better.

Walking back to the house, she went by the *Logger* office. Through the big window she saw the young fellow she had met at the Greek's earlier in the week. He was typing and he looked intent. She waved at him but he didn't look up from the machine. It was all right waving at him. He wasn't a customer.

— XIV —

SEWARD

GALE SEWARD crumpled a piece of copy paper and lobbed it at the big wastebasket by the society editor's desk. It went in and he felt a little better.

He tried again on the typewriter but only finished a couple of sentences before it seemed wrong and he wadded the paper. This time he missed the basket.

He was disgusted with himself. When the Boss had told him the night before to write an editorial about the inquest he had welcomed the assignment. He felt like teeing off on Coroner Jones. But when it came to writing what he thought, when he sat down at the Underwood with the blank paper sticking up over the platen, that was something else: he couldn't get his anger down on paper. He kept pulling his punches, qualifying his phrases, weaseling his verbs. He tried too hard for the appearance of fairness.

He worked on the inquest for another hour, but it was no use. At last he gave up, clipped an editorial in praise of stamp collecting from the sheaf of prefabricated, guaranteed inoffensive opinion sent by the national syndicate to all member papers, marked it to be set two columns wide in ten-point type on a twelve-point slug, put it on the spindle for the printers, and went out to eat.

Over the blue-plate special at Mother's Inn he admitted to himself what the trouble had been. He still did not want to take sides. He did not care deeply enough about the inquest to break the rules of the newspaper game as he played it. He did not want to print his emotions as facts. The subjective editorializing indulged in by Joe Kalinen and the Boss, he regarded as journalistic masturbation, stupid, debilitating, embarrassing; he was damned if he'd practice it. Reporting was the thing. He left his tip, paid his check, and walked down along the river to Logger Hall.

The big room on the ground floor was crowded with loggers in their Sunday suits and wet oxfords, back from the funeral. They told him he'd probably find the officers upstairs.

Leo Plotch, Arne Toivenen and Jack Winter were in the office. They were not glad to see him. He asked where Dawson was. They looked at each other for a moment before Toivenen said, "He isn't here."

"Where could I find him?"

"What do you want him for?" This suspiciously.

"I want to get a statement from him about the inquest. I tried all day to reach him. It sort of looks to me as if Jones is giving him the works and I want to get a statement from him."

"If you think it's a frame, why didn't you say so in the paper this morning?"

"We just ran what happened at the inquest. We didn't vouch for its accuracy. If we didn't run what went on there, it would be censorship."

"It's censorship not to say it's a frame."

"No. To say that would be editorializing. That's a matter of opinion."

They couldn't see his point of view on that at all. But after a time they believed in his good intentions; at least, they believed in him enough to admit they didn't know where Bull had gone after the funeral. He had left the cemetery in the car with the minister and they had not seen him since. If they located him, they would have him call the paper.

Seward said thanks, put on his hat, heavy and shapeless

with rain, and left. Toivenen caught up with him in the main hall. "Got time for a beer?"

Seward said he had. Toivenen took him to a small beer parlor a block from Logger Hall. It was a tiny place run by a huge Finnish woman.

"Ever been here before?" Toivenen asked.

"This is one I've missed. I thought I'd been in them all." He looked around the small room. "Lord, but this place is clean."

Toivenen was pleased. "She's a real old-fashioned Finn, all right." He slid onto a bench behind a squat, heavy-planked table with no initials carved on it. The proprietress brought two outsized muggs of beer and thumped them down. As she walked away Toivenen nodded toward her and said to Seward, "Scrubs everything in the place twice a day and does the sidewalk out front every morning, if it doesn't rain. Now listen." He reached over and put a nickle in the juke box. The lights flashed garishly, but when the music started it was somber, a symphony orchestra. "Sibelius," Toivenen said; " 'En Saga'."

"Damnedest place I ever saw," said Seward. "A juke box like that is going to ruin my plan to make a million bucks. I've been going to invent one where you put in a nickle to start it, but you can shut it off by putting in a dime."

Toivenen raised the mug. "Here's to the silent juke box."

The beer was excellent. Or perhaps, Seward decided, it was just the place and the music. "Is Sibelius a favorite of yours?" he asked Toivenen over the second beer.

Toivenen looked at him blankly for a moment, then smiled faintly. "You mean, do I let my political dislike for old Finn nationalism interfere with my feeling for Finnish music?"

"Something like that."

Toivenen's smile spread up toward his eyes. "I like Sibelius. But I like Shostakovich better."

They talked some more about music. Seward, who had always thought of Toivenen as a political symbol, neatly packaged and easily dismissed, under the label of communist, began to warm to him as a human being. The guy was well read, and his taste in American literature paralleled Seward's: he liked Steinbeck and Hemingway, couldn't stomach Wolfe or Saroyan.

"You ought to be a reporter," he told Toivenen, meaning it as a compliment.

"Not me." Toivenen said it too flatly.

"You don't think much of reporters?"

"Reporters are all right. It's just I wouldn't want a job where I had to take orders."

"You never get orders now?"

Toivenen's bulging eyes met his squarely. "None that I don't believe in."

"Hell, Pegler could probably say that."

"I'm not Pegler."

"Nobody said you were."

The spell was broken. The conversation that might have led to friendship turned formal. They were back to thinking of each other as editor and agitator, and their talk became a contest; they batted words back and forth at each other across the invisible net of their prejudices, seeking to score points rather than to reach understanding.

Seward's convictions were less deeply rooted than Toivenen's, and far more vague. He found himself on the defensive, and as the talk went on he grew angry at Toivenen's extravagance of expression. He objected to the epithets the agitator used.

Toivenen said, "If I see a man about to commit murder,

it is my duty to call the cops. And if I see the bosses about to commit fascism, it is my duty to sound the alarm."

"Bosses, fascism, murder. Jesus Christ, man, why do you have to talk like that? You sound like an editorial in *New Masses*. We're talking about people, not cartoons. I know Peterson and Gentry. I've interviewed them both, a number of times. They're reactionary as hell, yes. They hire people, sure. But they don't suck blood. Their canines don't hang over their lower lips. They didn't stop being human beings when they became businessmen."

Toivenen finished his beer and slid out from behind the table. "I'm sorry if I rubbed you the wrong way," he said. "You must forgive me. I'm a little upset. You see, somebody killed the wife of a good friend of mine. And now somebody is trying to send my friend to prison. That somebody might even be a human being."

He paid for the drinks and walked out.

Gale Seward finished his beer by himself, then ordered another. It was six o'clock before he left the tavern.

He walked back to work, a little drunk and very troubled.

— XV —

THE OLD MAN

THE old man sat in a booth at the bus station lavatory and counted the money in the purse: two ten-dollar bills, four one-dollar bills, a quarter and two nickels.

It had been so simple. He had just taken it. When he walked onto the bridge he had no money, and when he reached the other end he had twenty-four dollars and thirty-five cents. He could do that again. Any day. He should have thought of it before. He put the bills in his shirt pocket and the coins in his hip pocket.

He was still breathing hard from the run. He waited in the booth until his breath was steadier. The purse he crammed down to the bottom of the can for used paper towels. As he straightened up from the wastebasket he was startled by his reflection in the mirror; when he realized it was himself, that he had not been apprehended, the apparition smiled back at him from the glass. He ran his fingers through his tangled hair, caught some water in his hand and pushed it against his face, then sponged up with a dirty towel. With bloodshot eyes he checked his appearance again in the mirror and found it good.

The liquor store was a block down the street. The short line at the counter moved with agonizing slowness. A soldier at the head of the line, a master sergeant with hash marks to his elbow, tried to kid the clerk into selling him "some of the good stuff under the counter." The soldier left, the line moved up a notch, and a housewife debated the difference between brandy and Southern Comfort, deciding at long last to get Rock and Rye, just for a lark. The man ahead of him bought whiskey and left. And there he was at the counter with the clerk looking at him. "Bottle of gin, bottle of whiskey."

"What brand?"

"Cheapest you got." Then he remembered how much money he had. "No, make it the best."

"You mean the most expensive?"

"Yah, the best."

"Your permit?"

"Huh?"

"Your liquor permit."

He remembered where the permit was—back at the shack. But he searched wildly through his pockets, hoping the clerk would say it didn't matter. Finally he admitted, "I left it to home. I'll take out another."

"Can't do that, pop. It has to go through regular channels."

"Then give me the cheapest."

"What?"

His hands were shaking. "Give me the cheapest instead of the best."

"Look, pop, I can't sell you anything without a permit. Cheap or good. State law."

"Some wine."

"Sorry, no can do."

"Dammit, gimme something to drink."

"Just a second, pop, be right with you." The clerk walked to the far end of the counter, ducked through a tunnel, and came out on the customer's side. He went to the old man. He put a hand on his shoulder and steered him, firmly and gently, through the door. The clerk was used to this sort of thing, though he thought, "Jesus, it's still afternoon and not even a weekend and the place is crawling with characters." The old fellow looked as though he were going to cry. The clerk felt sorry for him: some rummy in from the sticks, just to get tanked up, and here he'd gone and forgotten his card. Well, he could always drink beer. Wild-looking old bastard, but no harm in him, probably, no harm at all.

"You can't even sell me no gin?"

"Sorry, pop, it would cost me my job." He really did feel sorry for the rummy, but hell, he couldn't go sticking his neck out and selling without a card; they could check on that. "Don't you know where the bootlegger lives?"

The old man's face brightened. He had forgotten the bootlegger. "Schoolteacher Johnny's."

"That's it, pop. So long." The clerk went back into the store and his rejected customer lurched off toward the town bootlegger's establishment.

Schoolteacher Johnny's was a very respectable speakeasy. John Linchamber had opened it a year after the repeal of prohibition; twelve years of trying to teach Civics to ninth-graders had left him exhausted spiritually and financially, so when a bootlegger he knew casually asked if he would like to be an outlet for extra-legal liquor, he jumped at the chance. As soon as he was certain business would be good despite repeal, he resigned from his school post. He was a dull and timid man and wanted to avoid scandal. Johnny and his wife, Clara, a prim Canadian woman he had wooed and won during a ten-day spring vacation in Victoria, sold their bottled goods at exactly twice the state prices; they offered mixed drinks at a flat seventy-five cents apiece, extended no credit, paid their protection and attended church regularly, and had no public troubles. There had never been a fight in Schoolteacher Johnny's, it was that dull; and of course there had never been a raid. When business was quiet, Johnny wrote on a civics textbook he was preparing in long-range collaboration with a professor at Northwestern.

Most of Schoolteacher Johnny's customers went around

to the back door. It was necessary to knock and wait to be let in, and they found it less conspicuous to wait on the lattice-framed back porch than on the front porch, which was exposed to Elm Street. But the old man walked right up and pounded on the front door.

The door was opened by Johnny, a round, pink-faced man whose eyes behind protecting pince-nez were surprisingly cold.

"I wan' whiskey and gin."

"That would be twelve dollars and forty-eight cents," said Johnny, a quick man with figures; his tone implied that he did not think his customer had anything like twelve dollars.

The old man fished the folded bills from his shirt pocket.

Johnny stepped aside, let him into the house. The old man waited in the parlor while Johnny got the liquor. He looked around the room without really seeing. It was like almost any parlor in Cove, except that there were three sofas instead of the usual one. There were also a leather chair, an upright piano that Johnny had muted to the point of inaudibility, a couple of upright chairs and that was all, except for pictures of George Washington crossing the Delaware and Johnny's brother-in-law in the uniform of the Royal Canadian Air Force.

Johnny came out of the kitchen with the bottles in a paper sack and with fifty-two cents change in his left hand. The old man paid him, a ten and three ones, and took the sack and the change. He pulled the bottles from the bag to look at them. "Can I sit around here with one?"

Johnny looked with unconcealed disfavor at the plaid shirt and work pants, wet from the rain and muddy from the night under the bridge. But the old man still had a ten dollar bill in his hand. Johnny said, "Come on out in the kitchen."

The kitchen was large. The house was old-fashioned, but it had been re-equipped since Johnny changed to a more profitable profession. Around two walls were ranged an electric stove, refrigerator, tabletop automatic hot-water heater and a combination washing machine and dishwasher. The third wall supported a small bar and from the fourth protruded a chrome-trimmed, plastic-topped table, on which the proprietor had spread notes for a chapter in his proposed civics textbook.

There was only one chair, and that was by the table. The old man sat on the floor in the space between the range and the hot-water heater, and he drank gin straight from the bottle.

From time to time Johnny looked up from his notes and told a story. He talked mostly about customers. "A woman was in here a while before you came and she asked if I had any Chilean Reisling, said she couldn't get any at the liquor store. And I said, 'Madam, I know what you mean. It comes in a green bottle like a vase and I haven't got it.' She was provoked and asked why I did not have it. And I said, 'Madam, most of my customers want to know has it got a cork or has it a screw top and they take the screw top because they can get it open quicker.'"

The old man was a poor audience. He was drinking hard, taking the gin in hurried gulps. He was beginning to remember things and he was concentrating on getting drunk.

Someone interrupted one of Johnny's stories by knocking on the front door. The bootlegger left the kitchen. The man at the door was Bull Dawson. Johnny let him in and escorted him to the leather chair and brought him a whiskey at once. He had had Bull in junior high school and he was sorry for him. Dawson was taking this business hard, and Johnny, who loved his wife, understood. He did not offer any sympathy other than the whiskey, and he did not ask to be paid on delivery. He withdrew discreetly, but he drew a line on a sheet of paper to signify that Dawson owed for one drink.

Around eleven o'clock Johnny's wife came downstairs to cook their lunch. Johnny was working up his notes on the Proportional Representation system of voting, which he thought would cure most of the world's political ills. Dawson's score stood at seven drinks. Bull was staring drunk, but quiet. The old man was also drunk, but he was talking to himself. Most of his words were unintelligible, but those Clara could make out offended her.

With Johnny's help she hoisted him to his feet. Johnny tucked the bottle inside the top of the old man's pants, cinched up his belt, and together they steered him out the door.

He did not protest.

They shut the door behind him and he shuffled down the alley, cursing to himself.

— XVI —

SAFEWAY

CHIEF OF POLICE SNOW pushed a pair of baskets on wheels between the rows of canned goods in the super-market. He walked absent-mindedly past the bottled ketchup his wife had twice reminded him to bring home. His mind was not on shopping.

Twenty-five thousand dollars was a lot of money. The Chief knew that if Bill Elliott had twenty-five thousand his impertinence would ripen into mutiny and then he would quit; but if Elliott didn't get the money, he would talk. The Chief felt he should be pleased that Gentry's money stood ready to buy him out of the Barovich trouble, but he was not pleased; he did not want to make thousands of dollars for Bill Elliott. But if he didn't . . . His thoughts teeter-tottered on the problem of Elliott: to give, or to be betrayed.

"Say, Mr. Snow." It was the store manager speaking, a bald young man of about thirty, who had recently been transferred to Cove from Grays Harbor by the grocery chain. "I wanted to tell you that I think someone tried to break in here last night."

"Yeah? What makes you think so?"

"There are dents on the storeroom window sill, like someone tried to jimmy it."

"Yeah? Let's see."

The bald young man led him to the storeroom; he looked through the rain-streaked pane at the dented sill, then went into the alley and examined it. Someone had certainly worked on the window with a pry-hook. There were dents on the outer edge of the sill and at the bottom of the frame. "You sure these were made last night?"

"Very sure." He had a precise way of speaking that irritated Snow. "I check each morning on these things. I thought you ought to know."

"Yeah, thanks. I'll tell the guy on the beat to keep a closer watch on the joint."

"That will be fine."

They walked back to the counter together. But Snow was mentally miles away. He had seen a solution to his problem.

He went home without buying the ketchup.

Later that afternoon the Chief drove over to the Elks club. It was a little before five. The bar was deserted except for the Finn barkeep, who was reading the *Chess Review*. Snow played the slot machine until, exactly at five, Gentry came in.

They ordered drinks—a martini for Gentry, a rye and soda for Snow—and took them into a corner. They were alone except for the barkeep.

"Well?"

Snow shook his head. "He's not having any."

"At any price?"

"At any price."

"He say why?"

Snow shook his head. "I think he wants my job more than anything. He can get it if he sounds off, he thinks."

"Looks bad for you."

"Not me. I'll pinch Barovich."

Gentry finished his drink. "Okay. What is it?"

Snow raised his eyebrows.

"What's your angle? Even if you can get out, you don't want your boy talking out of turn."

Snow nodded agreement. "Is that property you spoke of

last night available for anybody who shuts Elliott up?"

Gentry tried to find some more liquor in the little glass in his hand, but there wasn't any. He called to the Finn for a double brandy, and before it came he said to Snow, "I don't like it."

Snow aimed his chin at Gentry. "I don't either. But it's a way out."

The Finn came over with Gentry's brandy and they were quiet until he was back at the bar.

Gentry tossed down the brandy and shuddered. "I wouldn't okay it."

"But if someone acted without your okay?"

There was no emotion in the clean-cut face of the coolest player ever to appear in the Rose Bowl. He looked at the Chief with businesslike blankness. His thoughts were chaos: the Chief's words slid across the surface of his mind, and though their meaning was unavoidable they did not burr into his consciousness. It was easy for Gentry to say, "That would be different."

Ordinarily Bill Elliott would not have arrested him. Unlike the other Cove cops, he did not enjoy making arrests; they gave him no sense of triumph. But he was in a bad mood: the night stretched ahead for hours, the rain was cold, his fingers already ached. And the old man stood there right under the street light, urinating.

Even then Elliott might have let him go with a bawling out if the old geezer had not been so drunk. He could not take care of himself. He could not even say where he lived. If he let the old goat go he might walk off the dock or go to sleep on the railroad tracks or some damned thing. So he ran him in.

The station was warm. The Chief wasn't around, nor were

the prowl-car crewmen. It was pleasant to be inside. Elliott liked the night desk sergeant, and they took their time booking the old man. He wouldn't give his name but the night sergeant recognized him.

"It's old Freitas from down at the beach." He went to the card file and came back with a drawer. "Sylvan T.-for-Tecumseh Freitas." He shook his head. "With a name like that you've got burdens enough, eh?" he said to the old man, who was holding the edge of the desk with both hands and rocking back and forth, too drunk to comprehend.

Elliott copied the name on the booking blotter. "Got his age?"

The sergeant checked the card. "Sixty two years ago. I mean two years ago he was sixty. He looks a million and two, don't he?"

Elliott wrote down the age. Under the charge he put *Ind Ex,* for indecent exposure.

They went through the old man's clothes. They found a bottle of whiskey, eleven dollars and eighty-seven cents, a key-winding gold watch inscribed "To my son on his 21st birthday," an outsized jacknife with a blade beyond the legal length, a billfold containing a pornographic picture, a plug of snoose, and some agates from the beach. The sergeant put the money in an envelope; and the envelope, along with the other treasures, except the whiskey, he placed in a cigar box.

The sergeant unlocked the door to the cell block. "Come on, old-timer."

The old man let go of the desk and half sat down, half collapsed to the floor.

"Get up and come on."

The old man said something they could not understand, but his tone put the idea over.

Elliott grinned. "Okay, junior, time to go beddy-by." He stopped, picked the old man up under one arm and, balancing the weight on his hip, hitch-stepped to the cell block.

"He going to need the soft one?" the sergeant asked.

"I don't think so. Anybody in the tank?"

"Nary a soul."

"It'll do, then." Elliott carried him into the drunk tank, a square room, bare except for a low toilet crouching in one corner. He laid him on the floor.

The old man glared at him from the floor; his eyes were bloodshot and saliva ran from the corners of his mouth into his stubbled beard.

The sergeant said, "I don't think he likes us."

"He'll like us less in the morning when old Knox fines him that ten bucks." Elliott left the tank, and the sergeant locked up. "Anyway, he'll be safe in there. It's a bitch of a night out."

"When you going to get off the corn patch?"

"Ask the Chief."

The sergeant, though he liked Elliott, did not want to get involved in force politics. He changed the subject. "Nothing doing tonight?"

"Pretty quiet."

"See the parade this afternoon?"

"I slept in. What parade?"

"Funeral of that Dawson gal. Jeez, there was a million cars and more damn loggers marching behind than come to town over the Fourth. They came right by our place on the way out to the boneyard. My old lady woke me up to see it. Damn near enough to scare you, Bill, I'm telling you, all those guys walking through the rain as though it wasn't there at all. Zombies, damn near. Gave me quite a turn."

"They do anything?"

"Nothing except march. That was enough. It sure was something. Never saw anything like it."

"Who organized it?"

"Nobody, far as I know. No permit for a parade or anything. Course you don't need one for a funeral. I had a time getting back to sleep, I tell you."

"Sorry I missed it. But I needed my shut-eye. I was all gooned out." He snapped his fingers softly. "Just remembered. Now I'll have to get up in time for police court tomorrow. If I'd remembered sooner I'd have let the old guy go."

"I can come in instead."

"No, thanks. It's Ind Ex, and I'll have to testify to catching him at it."

"Make it D and D. I can testify he was that."

"Aw, drunk and disorderly'd cost him a week in the pokey. What the hell. It won't kill me to get up at ten."

"A week in jail might do him good. He's going to need that long to sober up. I'll bet his piss is still a hundred proof tomorrow."

"A week might do all of us good, but we wouldn't like it."

"Well, we'd get fed, anyway." The sergeant glanced at the clock. "Time to put in the check with the prowler. I'm asking them to bring me a hamburg. Want anything?"

"Duty calls. There's some sidewalk needs walking on." Elliott shrugged into his slicker. He waited until the sergeant had made his short-wave check and then said, "Thanks for offering to come in for me. I appreciate it."

The sergeant settled himself in his chair. "And I appreciate your not taking me up on it. Ten o'clock. I'll be glad when this town gets big enough to have a night court."

"I should live so long. We've lost population on the last

two censuses." Elliott turned up the collar of his slicker, blew on his fingers, and went out.

He hated walking beat. For an hour, two hours, it wasn't bad, except on nights like this when it was miserable right from scratch. But after two hours, even on the best of nights his feet hurt, then his calves ached and before the end of the shift the muscles on his back were tangled. And it was so useless, keeping kids from chucking rocks through windows or shooting at street lights with air rifles, telling drunks to get on home, arresting old men because their kidneys weren't cast iron.

He wasn't cut out to be a cop. He had known that right from the start. When still in high school he wanted to be a fisherman. He haunted the docks, mooched rides across the bar at least every other day, and knew every fishing vessel that put into Cove; he could repeat the fishing gossip of the entire coast, and knew which boats had struck tuna off the Galapagos and which were taking salmon in the Bering.

Maybe he should have been a fisherman. But he had been a pretty fair catcher on the high school team; he handled pitchers well and hit a long ball. When he was offered an athletic scholarship at a little college in the eastern part of the state, his folks talked him into accepting it. A college education was the key to success. Four years he might have spent fishing—the best four years the deep-sea boats ever had—he spent getting a liberal education. Liberal education: an interest in unprofitable subjects and the sure knowledge he couldn't hit a curve. It was poor equipment for earning a living. By the time he graduated in 1931, fishermen could not get enough for their fish to pay for the cost of catching them. Baseball clubs were not hiring players who couldn't hit curves, and a B.A. from a hick college in the wheatlands was good for nothing.

So he took a Civil Service exam for the police force. He

did all right in the test. When the first opening came up, he was named. He was a natural: over six feet tall, weighing slightly more than two hundred, and popular with the high school kids because of his athletic record. The only trouble was he'd never liked it. He had intended to keep the job just a year or so, until something better turned up.

But Gwenn got tired of waiting for prosperity to round that corner. She told him it was marriage or nothing: they were married. But they never had any money. He didn't try to supplement his pay by any of the devices that were so usual they were almost legitimate. So he never got far enough ahead to quit. And what the hell, he didn't know anything except being a cop. Pounding beats hadn't taught him how to hit a curve, and his B.A. was worth no more now than when the prexy, looking very dignified in his black cape and mortarboard, handed it to him in that long-ago spring.

If he got to be Chief . . . But he didn't really want to be Chief except to win over Snow. It would be a pleasure to ream Snow. Snow would pop a hernia if he ever got to be Chief. But the Chief's work, hell, that would be a real headache.

Elliott reached the halfway point in his beat. He had noticed nothing along the way, and he was a little pleased that he hadn't. Snow could lead him out into the water, but he couldn't make him look. He phoned the desk and said everything was okay. The sergeant asked how was the rain. Elliott said it was dry.

He entered the part of the beat he liked best: the residential district. He was always jealous of the people on the cozy side of the panes, but he enjoyed looking into the houses. And not just for the occasional strip shows, though he was not unappreciative of such minor blessings. He simply enjoyed watching people live. Somehow, life always looked comfortable and complete, seen through a window.

He should have been a Peeping Tom. The idea pleased him and he toyed with it. Profession: Peeping Tom . . . Do you call that gainful employment? It's not a job, it's an art . . . But it's illegal. That's what I like about it.

And there was the real trouble. His sympathies were so much with the underdog that he preferred lawbreakers to officials. He hated authority; or feared it. He could remember the longing that came over him to smack the coach with a bat when the coach bawled him out for taking a third strike. But he hadn't hit the coach. And he hadn't told the prexy what he thought of his college. He had never even told his stepfather what he thought of him. Of course, the Chief knew. That stupid pig. By God, there was one symbol of authority he didn't fear. He'd fix him for fair at the inquest. Or, if he couldn't get a chance to testify there, he'd break things wide open at the next council meeting. By God, that would settle Snow.

He tried to figure out whether he hated Snow most as Chief or just as a person, but it was chicken-or-egg, finite-or-infinite, and he gave it up. Authority was necessary, he guessed; but by God, why did a little bit of authority turn a man into a bastard? You could beat your brains out on that one. He was still working on it when he saw the light flash in the darkened store.

He stopped short and waited.

The light glowed again, pink and dim, as though someone were shielding a strong flashlight with his hand. Then it went out.

Elliott walked backward so that the street light was between himself and the window. He hoped he had not been seen. He stood in the protection of the telephone pole and watched the window, waiting for the light to show again. He took his heavy revolver from its holster. The butt was cold and wet and did not reassure him; he hated the feel of guns.

He could feel the tension. His stomach was cold; the muscles were tight along the front of his legs and across his shoulders. He felt a little sick.

The rain was coming down very hard. The light did not show again. Whoever it was might have seen him. He'd be going out the back way, or maybe just waiting for him to go past. Elliott decided to play it straight. He walked backward for about thirty yards, then came swinging down the sidewalk in his regular stride. As he passed the storefront he flashed his light inside the window, a routine gesture, and tested the front door. The light revealed nothing out of the ordinary, and the door was locked. He walked on. Once out of sight of the front window, he ran around behind the building.

The back door was ajar.

Elliott hesitated. It was one block to the direct-line telephone to the station. For half of that distance he would be in sight of the building; no one could get away if they had not already escaped. But during the minute or more it would take to make the call, they could leave.

He very much did not want to go into the store alone. His heart was beating hard enough to hurt, and he knew he was afraid, terribly afraid. His mouth felt dry, and his Adam's apple was an unmanageable lump. He told himself it was silly, that the light might have been held by someone from the store. The electric lights might be on the blink and an electrician could be checking on it. Even if it was a thief, it woud probably be some school kid. But still he was afraid.

And the phone was a block away.

Elliott walked quietly to the door. He stood by it, listening, hearing nothing above the splash of the rain pouring down the spouts.

He opened the door gently, slipped through and stood against the wall in one corner of the great oblong of darkness. The windows at the front of the building were gray. Nothing moved against their light.

There was no sound, except the beat of the rain on the roof.

He rubbed his shoulders along the wall, feeling for the light switch. He could not find it. Carefully he extended his left arm so that it was well away from his body. He turned on the flashlight.

The beam bored a yellow hole through the darkness. It revealed a counterful of soda crackers. No sound, no movement. He played the light around the room and saw only a deserted store.

Slowly, still careful not to make a sound, though he kept the flashlight on, he walked to the front of the building. Nothing.

He came back along the next line of counters. On his left were breakfast foods. On his right, jellies. He noticed the price of strawberry jelly and thought it high. This struck him as ridiculous. He had to fight off an impulse to laugh.

He played the light on the wall, found the switch and turned on the store lights. Nobody moved. Everything was in order.

He remembered that he had not looked at the cash register. It was on the counter toward the front of the store. He started down the aisle.

Behind him a door squeaked. The storeroom, Holy Christ, the storeroom. He spun. Before he got all the way around there was a noise, not terribly loud, like the sound of a paper bag being burst, and at the same time something hit him on the side of the head. It hardly hurt at all.

Elliott was dead before he hit the floor.

— XVII —

POLICE COURT

THERE was a small light in the ceiling. The ceiling was miles away. The light was swimming in the ceiling like a trout in a pool; lazily, like a trout in a pool.

It made him dizzy, watching the light swim like that. He rolled onto his stomach. The floor was of linoleum. The linoleum was brown, and it was turning slowly, slowly turning beneath him. He tried to stop it with his hands. It spun on faster now, very fast. He shut his eyes, but the darkness whistled. He was sucked down into the vortex of the spinning darkness.

When he opened his eyes—how much later he did not know—the floor was steady. The linoleum was porous and grainy. He stared at it until the dots seemed to expand to the size of fish scales. He blinked, and they were grains again.

He sat up and looked at the ceiling. It was low and an electric globe was screwed into a socket set flush with the ceiling. The light was small and it glowed yellow.

Where was he?

He looked around the room. It was bare except for a toilet in the corner and a door with a small window. He got to his feet. Twin splinters of pain behind his eyes probed back into his head. He caught his forehead in his hand and stood bowed with pain. The pain faded, leaving him sick and weak. He walked to the door and leaned against it until he felt stronger. He looked out the little window. The window was screened. Through the heavy screen he saw a corridor lined with gray bars.

He was in jail.

Musta been awful drunk, he thought. He rubbed his hand over his bearded face and tried to remember. He'd been drinking, all right. He could remember sitting in a white enamel box, drinking. No, not a box, somebody's kitchen. He'd been drinking in somebody's kitchen.

With a rush it came back. He could not remember what happened after he was in the kitchen, but he knew what went before. He knew what they had arrested him for. Murder.

Not since he raised the iron in anger and brought it down on the girl's skull had the word *murder* come to him. But it had been there, all right, deep within him. And now, here in jail, he was filled with it. It pounded in his temples, rose and fell with his chest, rasped with his breath. The word filled him, smothered him, bound him. He was choking with it. He tried to force it from his lungs.

A face appeared at the window. "What's the matter?"

It was a cop. The cops had him. He was in jail. He didn't say anything to the cop.

"Got 'em bad, huh?" the cop said. "The little men crawling out of the woodwork, huh? That's what happens to you winos. Now cut the screaming and get some rest. If the judge gets the idea you're crawling, it'll go tough."

The face went away from the other side of the window.

Goddam cops. How'd they caught him? How'd they know he killed her? But it wasn't murder. It was an accident. He'd only meant to help her iron the clothes. She must have hit her head when she fell. That was how it was, hit her head. But the cops wouldn't believe that. Never in a million, billion years. Never gave a guy a chance. No chance 'tall.

How'd they caught him? What'd he done wrong? What'd he said? He tried to remember, but the pain behind his eyes stabbed at him again.

He sat on the floor, his back to the wall. He had to be cagey, he had to be so very cagey. He had to do it himself. In all the world there wasn't one person who'd stick up for him and tell the cops how it'd been, that she'd hit her head. Not a goddam person. Not one. Everyone against him. He had to do it all himself. He had to be smarter than them. He had to get out of this.

The old man crossed his arms on his knees and leaned forward. He was all alone, and he was so tired.

In another room, fifty feet away, Chief Snow leaned over the metal desk in his clean, windowless office and read the memorandum he had written on the subject of William Elliott's death. He had written it the night before, as soon as he reached the station. But he wanted to be sure it still read right:

This afternoon the manager of the Safeway Store, Third and Cedar, Mr. Robert Thornton, approached me in the store and informed me that there had on the previous night been an attempt to break and enter. Upon examining the window of the storeroom on the alley side of the Safeway Store I discovered marks indicating there had been such an attempt to break and enter. I informed Mr. Thornton that we would place the building under special watch.

Around ten o'clock this evening I left the Elks and drove home. After getting home I remembered that I had intended to make a personal check on the situation at the store myself. I had already put my car in the garage and as the rain has swelled the door so that it is difficult to open and shut it, and as the store is only three blocks from my home therefore I walked to the store. This must have been around ten-thirty.

When I arrived at the store I discovered the back door open and I looked inside. Somebody was prowling around in the store with a flashlight. I said, Come out of there. The light went out and there was a shot. I shot back at the flash of the gun and I heard him fall. I turned on my flashlight and saw that it was William Elliott.

I assume that Elliott was merely investigating after having noticed an open door, although it is difficult to explain why he fired at me. I telephoned the hospital and Dr. A. L. Sansich came immediately. He pronounced Elliott dead and that he had died immediately.

I returned to the station, turned in my revolver to Night Desk Sergeant Lawrence Allen, and asked Captain Verne Janssen to assume the duties of Chief of Police pending a complete investigation of this unfortunate accident.

Snow read it through a second time, just to make sure. It read the way he wanted it to; he had forgotten nothing, nothing except the date and he added that with a glance at the calendar. He held his long, blunt chin in the circle of thumb and forefinger, rubbing his thumb along the underside of his jaw and listening to the dry, scratching sound of his day-old whiskers. It had been an inspiration to fire Elliott's gun; that made the appearance of an accidental duel more authentic, much better than if just one shot had been fired. The only risk had been that someone might have been passing the store at that moment; he had gambled on that and, he believed, won. The sound of the shots had not carried through the storm. The crowd had not gathered at the store until the ambulance came.

It had gone precisely according to plan.

Snow stood up and stretched. He had had a good night's sleep. Only six hours, but it had been solid sleep, untroubled, and he felt fine, never better.

This one little thing changed everything. With Elliott dead, there was nothing to worry about. There was no one to say that Barovich had been arrested, no one except Barovich himself or the night desk sergeant, and the sergeant would never take a chance like that. There was no one to raise the question of why the prowl car had been sent out of town on the night Dee Dawson was killed. No one was in a position to make himself Chief by playing smart politics. It was a load off his mind.

He opened a drawer, took a cigar from a box, bit off the end and lighted it. The smoke felt good in his chest and he snorted clouds.

He went to the outer office. The day desk sergeant was sweeping the floor.

Snow asked, "What's the matter with the janitor doing that?"

"He won't be in until one, sir, and there's police court at eleven. Couple of speeders, one indecent exposure, and that Plotch guy."

"Who's inside?"

"Just the I.E. Old guy from down the beach. The others are bailed."

"Why don't you have the I.E. sweep out the place?"

"He's an old fellow, sir, and feeling rocky. He had the screaming meemies back a bit. Guess he was carrying quite a load when Elliott brought him in." The sergeant's voice trailed off; he had not intended to mention Elliott to the Chief.

Snow did not seem to mind. "Ah, the hell with that noise. Do the old bastard good to get some exercise. Let him finish the floor."

"It's all done, sir."

"Well, then, give him a rake and have him smooth up the gravel in the parking lot. You could drown in some of the pools out there."

"Yes, sir."

The Chief went out and walked over to the Elks Club. He hoped Gentry would be there. He wanted to talk to Gentry about the land that could be bought at a twenty-five-thousand-dollar profit.

The day sergeant went into the cell block. He unlocked

the tank. The old man was sitting on the floor. "Hello, old-timer, we got a job for you."

The glazed eyes showed no comprehension.

"You got a coat?"

The old man shook his head.

"Well, I'll fix you up with one. We want you to rake the gravel smooth out in the yard. Okay?"

The old man nodded woodenly.

The sergeant led him into the outer office, took an old coat from the closet and helped him into it, led him outside to the tool shed and handed him a fine-toothed rake, showed him what was to be done on the parking lot where the prowl cars stood, and left him.

The old man pulled the rake over the rocks, smoothing the surface of the parking lot. He worked mechanically, unthinking, for several minutes. It did not come to him at once that he was outside the jail, unguarded, unwatched. When he realized it, he suspected a trick: they were trying to trap him some way. He'd have to outsmart them.

Raking the gravel as he went, he worked his way to the corner of the building, stepped around it, and waited. No outcry. Still, they might be sneaking up on him. He'd show them. He went back around the corner and raked some more, down toward the station door, then back. Again he ducked around the corner. He leaned the rake against the brick wall of the city hall and stopped as though to tie his shoe string. If they came, all he was doing was tying his shoe. Nobody came. He peeked around the corner. The parking lot was empty. He hid the rake in the back of a cedar shrub, buttoned the borrowed coat up to his throat and walked away.

As he crossed the street he began to run. Running was wrong, he knew it was wrong, and he forced himself to walk, even to look in windows; and he walked deliberately as far as the bus station, where there was the protecting solitude of the lavatory.

He washed his face. The hot water felt good. He rubbed his warm, wet palms on the back of his neck. But as he dried himself with the paper towels he noticed the wastebasket, empty, and he was suddenly afraid.

They must have found the purse!

He stepped into the toilet booth and shut the door. Take it easy, take it easy. Don't get excited. He'd fooled them so far, and the purse didn't really matter at all, not at all. The thing to do was get out of town. He could take the bus, right from here. From here he could go anywhere, right now, never come back.

How much money had he left? He felt in his shirt pocket and found it empty. His hip pocket, empty. His front pockets, empty. And back over them all again, and all empty. He'd been rolled. Those goddam cops musta rolled him. The sons-o'-bitches had rolled him. Christ on a crutch, he'd have to walk. He'd walk outa town, that's what. They thought they could keep him from taking the bus by stealing his money, but he'd walk and fool them. Too smart for 'em. He was way too smart for 'em.

He left the booth, the lavatory, the bus station. He walked down the side street toward Elm. Nobody noticed him. Oh, they thought they were so smart, these people, but he walked right past them and they did not even know enough to look at him, these bundled-up women with shopping bags, these businessmen running awkwardly from door to door through the rain. They did not notice him, any of them, not even the big cop standing under the marquee at the movie house on the corner of Eighth and Elm.

He walked along Elm. He walked behind the woman for half a block before he thought of it. She was carrying a purse.

It was a red purse and she had it tucked under her left arm. In her right hand she held a heavy paper shopping bag. She was fat and wobbled as she walked. There would be money in that purse, enough to take the bus. The bus was faster than walking, and it would show those cops if he took the bus even after they had stolen his money so he couldn't take it. He quickened his pace. He walked very close behind her.

She looked around at him and walked a little faster. He speeded up too. She couldn't outwalk him. He was too fast for her. They were almost in the middle of the block. Now.

He grabbed the purse.

He ran back the way he had come. She was yelling. Stop Thief. Stop Thief. He was running, way too fast for them, looking for the alley that was sure to give him protection, wondering how much money there was in the purse, spending it, buying a suit, a house, a woman. . .

There was a pounding of feet behind him, a blow at the back of his legs, a crazy spinning moment as he floated through the air, then blankness of shock as he hit the pavement.

When he came to he looked up into the tight, angry face of the policeman.

"You going to make any trouble?"

He shook his head. He knew when he was through.

Gale Seward lay face down on his bed, listening to the alarm clock. The alarm died out, and he still lay there, awareness nagging at him, sleep surging back up at him. Down the hall a door slammed. Outside a truck honked. He hoisted himself to his elbow and checked the clock's time against his wrist watch. They agreed that it was ten. He rolled over, swung his legs over the edge of the bed, put his feet on the floor and shuddered awake as the cold mounted through him. He slung a towel over his shoulder and, in his pajamas, went down the hall to the shower.

The hot water was barely warm, and it soon ran cold. He got out of the shower still soapy and went back to the room.

He felt miserable. It had been after seven when he went to sleep. Less than three hours. His face felt like a parchment mask. As he rubbed down with an old Army towel he looked at the headline topping the *Logger* that was spread on the floor:

COVE POLICEMAN SLAIN

Still true. The chair that he braced his foot on as he blotted the water between his toes was the chair Bill Elliott had sat in only three nights before. The glass Elliott had taken his wine from was still unwashed. The rain that Elliott had gone out into was still falling. But Elliott was dead.

Elliott's death was one hell of a fine story. No denying that. No comfort in it, either. The story had broken after the radio station signed off, but Seward could get no satisfaction out of the *Logger's* second exclusive of the week.

He felt responsible. He shouldn't, but he did. His reasoning was involuted and emotional, he knew that, but he could not avoid the conviction that if he had done as Elliott asked, the big cop would still be alive.

All through the night he had tried to evade his sense of guilt. He had run the story of the shooting almost as Joe Kalinen turned it in. He avoided the police station. He had not gone to the Greek's for his after-work coffee, but instead crossed the bridge to a little all-night restaurant in the Croatian district where he was not thought of as a newspaperman.

Then he had gone home and to bed, but not to sleep. He had read. He traced the pattern in the wallpaper, played leapfrog over the fleur-de-lis in the curtains, and recited passages from *Lady of the Lake* to himself, but he had been awake when the alarms began to ring in other rooms at six-thirty, and was still awake at seven when the neon sign outside his window went dull and ceased its spluttering. Only three hours' sleep.

He dressed slowly. The clock on his typing desk said ten forty-five when he left the room. He had time only for one cup of coffee before walking to the city hall to attend police court.

A police judge may be a young politician on his way up or old lawyer in need of money. George Knox was seventy, but he needed no money. A retired lawyer, he ran for police judge because he felt that the post needed a good man, and, quite rightly, he considered himself to be eminently qualified.

He was long past finding the pleasure of Solomon in his duties on the bench. Most police-court cases were routine. He handled them with as little bother as possible. He was always delighted when offenders failed to appear in court and he could close a case by ordering bail forfeited. He considered the court a necessary nuisance to himself and the community. The less fuss the better.

Arriving at the station five minutes before the hour, Judge Knox found more than a hundred men crowded into the space around the square maple desk that served as his bench. His first thought was that the Chief must have launched another traffic-safety campaign without warning him. The idea was not pleasant: traffic drives meant that the Better Element would get more than its share of tickets since it had more than its share of cars; when the Better Elements got tickets, it wanted the tickets fixed, and though Knox did not care how many tickets the Chief took care of (he was long past believing in the perfectibility of a police force) he would not fix them himself. This lost him friends; or, more precisely, speaking acquaintances sometimes stopped speaking to him. His friends knew better than to ask.

He paced through the crowd to his desk, placed his coat and hat across the far left corner, and seating himself, studied the docket. Only four cases: parking by a fire plug, jumping a stop light, disorderly conduct, and indecent exposure. He looked up at the crowd, nearly all men, laborers, uneasy in the presence of the law. If they were not here because they had been trapped driving their automobiles at twenty-seven miles an hour or more, or leaving them in one place for sixty-two minutes, they must be friends of one of the defendants. He checked the names: Meade, Liebig, Freitas, Plotch. It would be Plotch. He looked at them again, husky fellows most of them, loggers probably. Yes, friends of Plotch.

Judge Knox went into the Chief's room to check with the police. They always gave him the background on cases on the day's docket; he found it helpful to know a bit of the background of the defendants.

Three men were waiting for him in the Chief's office: the desk sergeant, Patrolman Haarka and Xenophon Jones. They said hello all around.

"Is our overflow audience a result of the proceedings against Leo Plotch?" Knox asked.

"Yes," the desk sergeant said.

Patrolman Haarka said, "I didn't realize I was running in Mr. Popularity himself. Have you seen the leaflets, Judge? I'm a Gestapo." He handed Knox a pamphlet:

FREE SPEECH DENIED

Gestapo Tactics
Police Arrest Plotch

Who Is Jones Shielding?

Knox said, "Who is distributing these?"

Haarka smiled. "Are you kidding?"

"No, I'm not joking."

"Well, Plotch's union, I suppose. But you know how it is with this sort of thing. Some kids were passing them out and they said a guy in a car gave them four bits to pass them out. Never saw the guy before, of course. He's probably only daddy."

"They are trying to intimidate me," Xenophon Jones put in.

Knox looked unsmilingly at the coroner. "From what I have heard of your conduct of Dawson's inquest, any attempt at intimidation would be what turn about is generally considered to be."

Jones showed his surprise. "That was what I came to talk to you about, Judge. The inquest is to be resumed this afternoon, and if you do not make an example of Plotch, I fear for the dignity of my court."

"You aren't holding court, you're conducting an inquest," Knox said snappishly, "and its dignity isn't a matter of concern to anyone but yourself. Further, I resent your approaching me in this manner."

"But as one official to another. . ."

"As one individual citizen to another, you are a fool and a mountebank." Knox turned his back on the coroner. The policeman were shuffling their feet in embarrassment. He asked them, "Is there anything I should know about the cases on the docket?"

Haarka grinned. "If you want me to say anything about Plotch, Judge, you gotta coax me."

"With a regular official, it is different."

Jones said, "I shall see that this is reported to the state bar association."

"You do that. And if you find anyone who will accept a report, there will be two of us making reports."

The desk sergeant said, "This man Freitas, who's up for indecent exposure, he's run off."

"Was he on bail?"

"No, we had him raking the parking area and he ran off."

"You aren't supposed to work them if they haven't been sentenced."

"The Chief told me to."

"I'll take it up with him."

"That's okay with me, Judge; but about this Freitas. He ran away, but I don't quite know what we could do about him anyhow. Bill Elliott was the arresting officer."

"Oh, I see."

"We have his stuff here, Judge—Freitas's. There's a little more than ten bucks in the box. Maybe we should set bail at ten, let him forfeit and forget the whole business."

"It's irregular," Knox said, looking grimly at the desk sergeant, who was used to him and stared back evenly; "but it appears to be a just and equitable solution. Is there anything else?"

"Not a thing."

"After you, gentlemen." Knox followed them into the outer office. More spectators had come in. He recognized several of them.

Leo Plotch was at the back of the room with the lawyer, Al Addison. Knox went to Addison and said, "I'll run through the routine cases first. It is unlikely to take more than five minutes."

"That will be fine, sir."

Knox eased himself into his chair, took the gavel from the middle drawer of the desk, and rapped it. The quiet was immediate. He let it last long enough to be impressive.

"It is unusual for a police court case to draw spectators," he began. "There is, of course, no objection to your presence. The normal processes of democracy call for our judicial actions to transpire publicly. I realize that there is on today's docket a case which has particular interest for one class or group in the community. I consider it probable that this case accounts for your presence. It is therefore possible that there exists among you a partisan feeling. I must ask that you refrain from expressing your emotions during the progress of this trial. Your function must be that of auditors, not of participants. I remind you of this simply because I assume that most of you are unfamiliar with the court prodecures of all types, even this merest utensil of justice—the police court. Should you feel that justice is not being served, you have recourse to higher courts." He paused. "If you have any questions about your rights, I shall be glad to attempt to answer them now."

There were no questions.

The judge picked up the docket. "Milton Meade. Parking within the proscribed limits of the fire plug at Seventh Street and Elm. Milton Meade." The desk sergeant, standing beside the judge, said, "Milton Meade." No answer. Knox rapped his gavel once and said, "Bail forfeited." He made a note of it on the docket.

The door at the far end of the room opened. Verne Janssen came in, holding an old man by the arm. He looked around the crowded room, saw that the desk sergeant was busy, and leaning across the booking desk, took out the booking journal.

Knox called, "Howard Leibig. Driving through a red

light at Fourth and Elm in violation of City Ordinance 12-312. Howard Leibig." The desk sergeant echoed the name. Knox rapped his gavel. "Bail forfeited."

He looked down the list of names, skipped over Plotch's, and said "Sylvan Tecumseh Freitas. Indecent exposure. Sylvan Freitas."

The desk sergeant repeated it.

The summons came from far away. The old man heard his name called. He walked toward the speaker, pushing gently between the spectators, who stood silently, their feet apart, waiting.

The judge had white hair. He looked stern. The old man remembered a hymn about the wrath of God. He hesitated, then shuffled to the edge of the desk. The judge was looking at him now. The judge was very near, and he seemed angry.

"Well?" the judge said.

"I'm Syl Freitas."

The policeman who had brought him to the station came up behind him and grabbed him roughly by the arm. "He's nuts, your Honor. I just nailed him grabbing purses down on Elm Street."

The judge looked at him, less sternly, and asked, "Who are you?"

"I'm Syl Freitas."

The other policeman, the one standing beside the judge, said, "He's Freitas, all right, your Honor. He's the guy who ran away this morning."

The judge looked severe again. "Purse-snatching is a serious offense, Mr. Freitas. Have you ever been arrested before?"

It was like watching a movie and thinking of something else. The words he heard and the thoughts he had were separate. He was in two worlds, and though they revolved around the same sun, they were vastly different. He was living through the life that began for him in that girl's kitchen; they were asking him about purses. He wanted to talk about that night. Something had gone wrong that night, and ought to be fixed up. If he told them how it was, they might understand. His lives might come together. The white-haired, angry man who looked like God might forgive him. They might let him sit down and rest. He wanted to rest. He was very tired. He leaned forward on the desk, supporting his weight on his knuckles. The room was beginning to sway before him, back and forth, back and forth, back and forth. He felt tired, he felt sick. It went on; the voices dimned, then grew loud, and he heard the judge say, "Are you guilty?"

He leaned back from the desk and stared at the stern face of the good judge, and he said, very slowly, "I killed her, Judge, but as Christ is my witness, I didn't mean to."

From far away the voice came, "Whom did you kill?"

"That girl in the kitchen. The blond girl." The judge's voice had been gentle, not angry, and the old man spoke rapidly, trying to tell him how it had been, trying to get it all said before the whirling world sucked him under, trying to see the judge through the spinning and speckled mist.

"She was ironing clothes and I wanted to help her and the iron it burned my leg. She was scratching at me too and I hit her with it, Judge, on the head. I can still feel it in my arm. It felt awful. And she just fell down there on the floor. I just wanted to help her. Only wanted to help her."

There was a rising sound behind him, angry and snarling, and he looked around at the whiteness of faces, faces that were nothing more than hot, angry eyes and tight mouths. He looked back at the judge, and the lone face was angry, too, and unforgiving.

"I didn't mean to do it," he said. "I didn't mean to do it."

The floor rushed up at him. He threw out his arms, but the floor brushed them aside and hit him in the face.

— XVIII —

THE LULL

THE rain abruptly stopped around mid-afternoon. Soon after, the wind warmed. Overhead the gray thinned, the sky took on depth as the opaque mass of cloud divided into layers that at varying speeds drifted landward from the sea and raised themselves over the deep green mountains.

When school let out, the boys walked home with their slickers folded over their arms, and the girls wore their coats loosely, like capes.

The storm was over, but still the river rose.

Far back in the mountains, where the root-knit earth held the water like a sponge and the shaggy bark of the evergreens was heavy with water, the creeks slowed and grew clear. But around the town lay the wasteland of stumps, and through this scarred land the water sluiced toward the Tala. Each denuded acre contributed to the flood. And when at last the stripped hills were free of water they were free, too, of tons of their scant soil. The stump ranchers, gaunt men worn thin by the struggle to redeem the wasted land, strode morosely over their rutted acres. They cursed the widening gullies.

The Tala rose, brown and turgid, powerful, threatening. On a bend above the town, a great rock washed out of the bank and the river rolled it downstream. The water swirled in the cavity, scouring it, enlarging it, cutting deeper into the soft earth behind, finally breaking through thinly in a new channel, swirling around a newborn island.

Upstream the river washed under the roots of a fir that

marked the boundary of an abandoned farm. Slowly, almost imperceptibly, the tree tilted. The strain on the anchored roots grew, and as they moaned a squirrel left the tree and bounded across the rutted field. A few roots sagged apart, but most held. Then the earth heaved around the base of the fir, and with a sighing rush the tree toppled into the river. The current pulled the tufted head downstream. The water ate the dirt around the exposed roots, taking it in great clods. And the fallen tree moved reluctantly downstream, catching at submerged rocks, at hanging branches, hesitating but then moving on, until at the bend above the town it swung into the new channel, clogging it, and for the moment the river turned back into its old course.

The river rose, but the wind was gentle and the tide was ebbing. The river stayed within its banks and the ocean absorbed the flood.

In town, the city engineer's crew checked the lids of the storm sewers, making sure none had been washed away. The road gangs for the railroad inspected the culverts. The district weather man studied his rain trap and telephoned headquarters that 1.31 inches had fallen in the previous twenty-four hours; at headquarters the information was received with some interest—it was the heaviest precipitation on the Coast for the period—but the meteorologists were more concerned with another storm three days to the westward.

Along Elm Street the merchants watched the water drain from the deep-curbed street, saw the sidewalks dry from slate to gray, and looking at the clearing sky, thought, "No flood, thank God."

— XIX —

LOGGER HALL

ARNE TOIVENEN stood in the darkened office on the second
floor of Logger Hall and looked down at the river. The re-
flections of the street lights lay like bars across the black
surface of the Tala, and the water slapped at the piles under
the building. Alone, Toivenen watched the river without
conscious thought.

And as he stood there the tension of the last week left
him, suddenly, too suddenly, like the air from a punctured
balloon. He could almost hear it whoosh. He felt collapsed,
let down.

A drink might help, but he decided against it. The bottle
was in the safe in the corner, but it was better to let it alone.
You could drink for companionship safely enough, but you
shouldn't drink to forget. Christ, look at Bull, tanked again,
and no more use to the organization than if Jones had gotten
away with railroading him. Less use, even. In prison he would
have been a martyr. But now, if he didn't snap out of it, he
was going to wind up just another dehorn rummy like the
old bastard who killed Dee.

Jesus! Some of the boys said the old guy was an ex-Wobbly
who'd slipped his trolley after one beating too many. Of
course, that was just talk and you couldn't be sure, but the
old goat might have been, at that. They'd sure been tough,
the Wobs. More guts than brains. What a hell of a way to
run a revolution, everyone running around being tough on
his own hook. Bunch of anarchists. No discipline.

Toivenen shook his head as he thought of the squandering of all that toughness.

But, Christ, they had been splendid, the Wobs. Even now you ran into guys who were reverent about them. They'd been licked, broken, buried—but damned if they'd been forgotten. That wasn't the way the bosses had figured it. Or the way the Wobs had figured it either, for that matter. You never could tell how things would turn out. You just couldn't tell.

Take Bull. Bull was the last guy you'd expect to go to pieces on a deal like this. And he'd split right up the middle. They'd broken Bull just as completely as if they'd made a Mooney out of him and shipped him to the pen. But they'd paid a price, Holy Christ, but they'd paid themselves a price for it.

There had been the funeral, and that had been fine. The funeral was good. There was sure something to be said for religion: it set the stage for planting ideas. The funeral was all right.

And the coroner had frigged himself right royally. Nothing Jones could do or say would make any union man forget the way he had worked over Bull. And now that Bull hadn't done it, everybody was going to be sorry for him and sore at Jones. It was good for authority to get caught with its pants down. The people had to get the idea that their officials weren't on their side; not under the system.

But what next?

Toivenen walked over and sat down at the desk. He was feeling better, and there was no need for a drink to give him a lift. What next?

Well, if Bull didn't snap out of it there'd have to be a new president. Plotch, probably. That wouldn't be so hot. Plotch was hard to maneuver. He was stubborn and independent, and though Bull could make him compromise he'd be a tough guy to handle as president. He was old. That would be a point against him. Maybe they could move young Koiva in there. The Finns would go for that, and Koiva's wife was a Norski and that would please the Scandinavians. He'd sound Plotch out on Koiva.

But Bull might not crack up. He might snap out of it. He should have something ready to suggest to Bull. There should be some follow-up to the inquest. It couldn't be the strike now. Christ, it was almost too bad the old bastard had confessed. If Bull had been railroaded they might have worked up something really good out of it. And that way Bull would have been useful. What would have been best would have been a successful frame, and then the old man's confession after he'd been there a few months.

But you couldn't have everything. You had to play them as they fell. The other side was still dealing. All you could be sure of was that they'd try to slip you the iron prod if you gave them half a chance. You had to be ready to turn their little tricks to your own advantage. If you expected the worst from the bastards, you weren't often disappointed.

He couldn't think of anything to do at the moment. He'd been thinking so hard about the sympathy strike it was hard to dismiss the idea.

But they'd try something before long. They always did. It would be clumsy, and he would be around to take advantage of their clumsiness.

He felt better now. It was all right to take a drink. He went to the safe and took out the bottle and poured himself a short drink. Before downing it, he put the bottle back and spun the dial. No use taking chances.

Bull Dawson sat on the edge of the bed and without interest watched Nellie step into her satin dress.

It had not been much good. A few drinks at Schoolteacher

Johnny's had convinced him that a woman was what he needed. But it hadn't helped.

"Can a guy get a drink here?"

"No. House rules." But she looked at him and felt sorry for him. All the way along she had known something was troubling him and had tried to make it good, but unsuccessfully, and so she said, "I could get you a glass of wine."

"Will you have one with me?"

"I don't drink on duty." This proudly, for it was a matter of much satisfaction to her.

"Ah, please."

"Okay, champ." She'd bring herself a glass. She wouldn't have to drink it. That, she knew. "Be back in a minute."

She went to the bathroom first, then to the kitchen, and poured two glasses of sherry from the bottle under the sink. She returned to the sad man who sat on her bed.

As she handed him the wine, he asked, "Do you know who I am?"

She shook her head.

"Dawson. William Dawson."

It meant nothing to her. She had read the story of the murder but, living outside of society, it had meant no more to her than a story datelined Boston or Shanghai. She said, "Oh, yes." Then, to be polite, "Do you work around here, champ?"

And that helped. He had imagined everyone was hanging on his troubles, exulting in them. It was a relief to have this woman accept his name unblinkingly, unaware of his notoriety. He drank his wine, then hers, and she refilled the glasses while he talked.

She did not pay much attention to what he said. She lost interest the moment he began talking about his wife. She had heard so much about so many wives, wonderful wives, terrible wives, two-timing wives, un-understanding wives. This guy had one of the good ones. She barely heard the old familiar phrases. "My wife is a wonderful woman . . . the only one I ever really went for, so that it meant something, you understand." She understood enough to nod, but her thoughts were far away. ". . .That business down in Portland, I wasn't really being unfaithful. It just sort of happened. It could happen to anybody." She said it certainly could, and gave him her glass again. He talked on and she sat, facing him, nodding when it was polite to nod, and from time to time raising her hand to her breast.

When Dawson left Snug Harbor he felt pretty good. He'd enjoyed talking to somebody who didn't tell him to do anything. She hadn't tried to talk him into anything, and she hadn't bawled him out.

He stood at the street corner for several minutes watching clouds stream across the face of the moon.

Then he walked to Logger Hall. He hadn't done any work for a week. He didn't know if he'd be much good, he felt so different. But he did feel like working.

— XX —

EDITORIAL MATTER

MONICA looked up from her book as Steve came in. Occasionally, perhaps three or four times a year, she saw her brother as a stranger, looked at him as she might a newcomer in church; and always she was surprised to find him handsome. Usually she was too busy worrying about what went on behind those dark eyes, what words were left unspoken by that wide mouth, what deeds were done by those big, long-fingered hands to think of what his features added up to. But today she noticed again that he was handsome.

Instead of going on up the stairs, he paused inside the doorway. He was smiling, and there was no mockery in it.

"You look happy."

"Do I?" He said it without challenge, rather as though he were surprised.

"Yes." She dropped her eyes to the book in her lap.

"Don't I usually?" He came over and sat in the worn chair next to the sofa. His long legs worked up over the arm and he leaned back on the other with his elbows.

"You haven't seemed happy for a long time, Steven."

But he changed the subject. "What you reading?"

She looked at the front of the book as though she needed to find out the title. " 'World Without End,' " she said. It was silly to be embarrassed: Steve could not know she had gone to the library looking for this book because Gale Seward had said it was the best he had read on the Balkans.

"Sounds deep."

There was no ready answer to that, for he might be mock-

208

ing her. She shook her head in denial, but he was not really interested in the book. "The radio been on this afternoon?"

"I turned it off before lunch."

"You haven't heard the news?"

"News?"

"They caught the guy who killed Mrs. Dawson."

She felt her eyes widen as she looked at him, and she felt the stiffness of her cheeks and the strain of her throat.

"It was some old guy who lives down at the beach."

"Really, Steven?"

"Sure, really."

So she sat there looking at her handsome brother, who had not killed Dee Dawson after all, who could lounge in the old chair and say casually this thing that cleared the family, say it as easily as though he were talking about the rain. And now that she did not need to shield him, she hated him, hated him for being the kind of person she could suspect of murder.

She did not know she was crying until he asked what she was crying about. Then she put her hands on her forehead and sobbed whole-heartedly.

After a while he said, "You thought I did it."

"No."

"So that's what you think of me?" She heard him stand up, but she did not look at him. She just kept on crying.

"So that's what you think of your brother." He was indignant. First there had been the relief, and then the necessity of telling someone. But now he could let himself go. He hadn't killed Dee Dawson, and it was a hell of a thing for his sister to think that he had. "A fine, loving family I have." He went upstairs. After he was out of sight she heard the hollow beat of his steps on the uncarpeted stairs, the slam of his door, and the creak of springs as he threw himself on the bed.

She cried a little longer, gently now, and then she went up to the bathroom and washed her face and replaced her make-up.

Steven hadn't done it.

If she met Gale again—when she met him again—there would be nothing they couldn't talk about.

She hummed "Kisa Pada" as she put on her raincoat.

Gale Seward braced his knees against the desk and teetered the chair on its hind legs. He toyed with the sensation of falling backward.

It was five-thirty and the office was empty. The bookkeepers had gone home, the sports editor was still at the Baseball turnout, the society editor was having dinner, and Kalinen was God knew where.

Seward had the place to himself. To his right the teletype chattered in its glassed-in room. He watched the machine spurt out the news in uneven bursts. It was working on a long story now, probably the night lead international, a summary of the world's major disturbances—catastrophe in a capsule.

Behind him the linotypes were impressing the history of the day on molten lead. They were working on society stories and advertising copy—early evening stuff—and the gliding fingers of the operators tapped out the chronicles of companionships that needed publicity to be enjoyed, and the price of cabbage.

He tilted the chair too far back and had to clutch the desk to keep his balance. He had to get to work. He settled all four legs squarely in their accustomed ruts and began to sort through the teletype copy.

But, even when working, he could not keep from thinking of Elliott.

Elliott had been wrong, just plain wrong. There was no

way around it. Steve Barovich had not killed Dee Dawson.

Gale felt faintly triumphant about that. He had not let the big cop buffalo him into running a story based on an unfounded rumor.

He wondered what Elliott would say about the old man's confession. Elliott wouldn't say anything about it. But if he were alive. . .

Oh, hell. He knew damned well what Elliott would say. He'd say that being wrong about Barovich didn't make any difference. Not the slightest. Dee's death had not been what upset Elliott. He was sore at a situation in which the cops accepted spying and blackmail as natural, maybe even indulged in a little themselves. Dee's death had only given him an opportunity to do something about that. And that situation was unchanged.

Mac, the make-up man, came in, swinging his wooden leg. "Any more killings yet tonight?"

"None so far."

"Chin up, stout fella. The evening's young." Mac took the copy off the spindle and went on out into the backshop.

Seward went into the teletype room and brought back a two-yard strip of stories. Anything to keep from thinking. He edited them carefully, rejecting, deleting, marking, writing heads, slugging. When he was finished he could not remember what the stories had been.

All right, the situation hadn't changed. Dee Dawson's death hadn't changed it. Neither had Elliott's. So what? He was a newspaperman, not a reformer. Nobody had hired him to change things.

He tried to imagine saying that to Bill Elliott. He had said something like that to Elliott once, and Elliott had been disappointed in him. Now the words sounded to Seward as they must have to Elliott: fatuous, stupid, false. But he would never have to say them to Elliott again. Elliott was dead.

And Elliott could not ask, Do you have to be hired to change things? What is your price?—the security of sixty a week? He was a writer. All right, was he afraid to write what he thought?

He rolled a piece of paper into the Underwood, looked for a desperate moment at its threatening blankness, and began:

"Bill Elliott was a brave man."

He wrote rapidly, unworried about organization or phrasing, wanting only to get it down on paper:

He hated injustice and he hated it enough to take a stand against it.

A few days before his untimely death, Bill Elliott argued with his superior officer about practices in the local police system which he believed to be dangerous.

He felt so strongly about matters of public interest that he risked the penalties of insubordination. He refused to stop thinking. He was exiled from the comfort of daytime prowler car duty to the ordeal of pounding a night beat. But he did not stop fighting against what he felt were abuses, at worst; or errors, at best.

Bill Elliott deplored the growth of private espionage and the extra-legal use of information obtained by legitimate agencies. In Elliott's opinion the Cove police were not as diligent as might be expected in suppressing industrial espionage. He was especially convinced that the homes of offices of union officials in this area needed additional protection.

He deliberately risked further punishment for insubordination—continued exile to the night beat he had patrolled when he first joined the force—to bring this matter to the attention of his superiors.

Bill Elliott thought that the police system of Cove needed a shake-up. He believed that only a complete overhauling would safeguard the rights of all our citizens. He felt that the relegation of union leaders to the status of second-class citizens where property protection was concerned was one of the main reasons for Delight Dawson's death.

Bill Elliott died a courageous death. He fell while carrying out his sworn duty to protect the property of Cove citizens. But, far more important, he lived a courageous life. He did more than his duty and, though penalized for his convictions, continued to exercise them.

Cove can ill spare such a man.

Helene Lewis came in from her supper. Seward rolled the editorial out of his typewriter and buried it under the teletype copy.

That was silly. He knew it. If he was going to slap this essay in the paper for all the town to see, he shouldn't be hiding it from a member of his staff. But the sense of it as his personal property was still upon him. Reluctantly, he took the editorial out and read it. He liked it. It wasn't going to win any Pulitzer prizes, but it got across the idea. And without libeling anybody. He hoped it was without libeling anybody. After all, if there was a suit the Boss would be the one to get stuck. There was nothing very noble about risking somebody else's property.

He read it again. It was a compromise. There were things he hadn't said. But they were things he could not prove. And this would be enough to raise a terrible stink. Baby, this would be more than enough. In the *Logger's* chaste editorial column, an editorial implying that the police winked at anti-labor spies would stand out like lipstick in a convent.

Mac came out of the backshop for more copy. "Still no murder, arson or rape?"

Gale handed him the editorial. "Read her and weep."

Mac read it through. "The Boss seen it?"

Seward thrust out his lower lip and shook his head.

"The Boss tell you to write it?"

"In a manner of speaking."

"He just told you to write an editorial?"

"Yeah."

"Don't you like working here?"

"Not if I can't get things like this off my chest once in a while."

Mac put the editorial at the bottom of the pile of copy he had taken from the spindle. "I'll set it myself. If Thomas sees it he may call the Boss."

"You think I ought to run it?"

Mac tapped the roll of paper against his bad leg. "I wish none of this had happened. All it has done is split the town farther apart than ever. But as long as these things have happened, I'm all for something like this." He looked down at the sheaf of copy. "It's what a paper is for." His eyes met Seward's. "Only I didn't think you knew it."

"I wish it were tomorrow morning right now."

"Tomorrow morning will be here soon enough." Mac went into the backshop.

Helene Lewis was looking at him oddly. He wondered what to tell her. But she spoke first. "What's between you and Monica Barovich?"

He didn't get it. "What?"

"You ask questions about her for about two days straight. And now she's parading by in front of the window. She's been by three times in the last five minutes, and you can't tell me she's looking in here just to see how I'm wearing my hair."

"No kidding." He ran to the door and stepped out. She was coming down the street. She saw him and stopped. He stood in the doorway, smiling.

"Imagine meeting you here," he said.

"I was just passing by."

"I'm glad. It saves me walking up and tossing pebbles at your window. I wanted to see you."

She smiled gravely.

"Let's have dinner," he said. "I've a lot to tell you."

She nodded.

He put his head through the door and called, "I'll be back," and then he turned to join her.

THE HOUSE ON THE HILL

RUTH PETERSON GENTRY watched her father eat breakfast with his napkin tucked in his collar. She had already plucked his spoon from his cup and laid it carefully in his saucer. She eyed him with distaste, hoping that he would note her disapproval and put the napkin in his lap.

Gordon Gentry, aware of the tableau, seemingly paid strict attention to his food. He wasn't sure which he wished more: that the old man would forget the old barrel-chested logging days, or that Ruth would stop trying to turn him into a parlor lizard. It just led to family fights. After the squabbles, Herm would hang around the office, first giving orders that weren't obeyed, then making suggestions, and finally retreating into the past and rolling anecdotes down upon his successors.

Well, it couldn't last forever. The old boy was slipping. Gordon had checked the insurance tables and the odds were against its going on more than seven years. He wondered whether in seven years Ruth could teach him her style of table manners.

Chimes sounded in another room. Ruth looked at her husband. "Are you expecting someone, dear?"

"No."

But the maid came and said there was a gentleman to see Mr. Gentry, a Mr. Snow.

Gentry told her to show the visitor into his den. After finishing his eggs, he excused himself.

The Chief was pacing the floor. His head was tilted forward so that his blunt chin rested on his chest, and his hands were in his pocket. A rolled newspaper stuck from his coat pocket.

Gentry said it was nice to see him.

Snow nodded, as though agreeing with the compliment, then said, "Have you seen the paper?"

"This morning's? No. It must be around somewhere."

"I have one." Snow handed Gentry the *Logger,* opened to the editorial page.

Gentry read Seward's editorial. His face did not reflect his surprise. He glanced through it a second time, partly to make sure he had read it correctly, partly to give himself time to think of its implications. Then, deliberately, he flipped the paper over to the front page and took a quick look at the headlines.

"Well?" Snow asked impatiently.

Gentry raised his eyebrows. "Well?"

"What's it all about?"

"I really couldn't say. Why don't you ask them at the paper."

"You put Olson up to writing that."

"Olson couldn't have written that. The sentences have verbs."

"Olson could tell somebody to write it. Seward, for instance. Olson could tell Seward. You could tell Olson to tell Seward."

"Why would I?" Gentry was genuinely surprised. But as he asked the question, he guessed the answer. Snow, with his relationship with Elliott under the faintest doubt, could not safely accept large amounts of money from anybody, not at this time.

The Chief said, "You're the only person who stands to gain by that editorial."

"You think I'd double-cross you for twenty-five thousand dollars?"

"Yes."

"I give you my word."

"Your word!"

"I will still buy the land from you."

"That's a mighty generous offer when you know goddam well I can't take money from you. Not now."

"I'll give you the money. Cash. No one needs to know."

Snow hesitated. He wanted the money very much. But for two hours, since the paper thumped on his front porch and, not sleepy, he padded out in bare feet and brought it back to read in bed, he had been in torment. He saw himself the victim of a neat double-cross. The belief that he had been tricked was deep within him. In any new offer, he suspected treachery. "I can't take money."

"No?"

"No. You know good and goddam well I can't. The inquest on Elliott has to be held yet. If Jones has any more ideas of making a hero out of himself, he might crucify me. And God knows what a grand jury will do. I can't go sticking twenty-five thousand dollars in the vault."

"Bury it in the back yard."

"You're humorous as all hell."

"You're hysterical, Roger."

"Who's hysterical? Goddam it, I see the whole thing. You managed it damn nice, didn't you, getting me to do your dirty work, then fixing it so you don't even have to pay off."

Gentry did not lose his temper. He had worried about the Elliott business after Elliott was dead. He regretted it. But he had a superstitious confidence in his snap judgments, and now it seemed another had worked out. Elliott was out of the way. Barovich was clear on the Dawson murder. And now Snow was in a spot where he couldn't take money. Not that the money itself mattered, but if he paid Snow anything, even on a land deal it would be an additional involvement. But if things stood as they now did, there was nothing. Only the veiled and ambiguous words spoken at the club the day Elliott died.

He looked the Chief in the eye. "Suppose that I did. What could you do about it?"

It was very quiet in the den. The lights shone dully off the mahogany and leather. The hum of an electric clock sounded unduly loud.

The Chief opened his mouth. He made little dry sounds. Twenty-five thousand was a lot of money to him. At last he said, "There's nothing I can do right now, but there'll come a time when you'll need me."

Gentry stood there, smiling faintly. He did not look as though he would ever need anyone's help again.

"Things break for you," Snow said. "Things break your way. But not always. Some day . . . Jesus Christ, will I ever pour it to you."

"I'll remember that." It was a long time since anyone had bawled him out, and Gentry did not like it. "Now if you have finished. . ."

Snow walked out.

He got into his car and drove very fast along the winding road down from Siwash Point. At the foot of the hill he stopped and looked up at the fine house fronting the bluff.

Twenty-five thousand bucks. Twenty-five thousand. And now, never again, peace of mind. Always the fear something would turn up. The worry of what was being said behind his back. And twenty-five thousand bucks gone. Just like that.

Gentry rejoined his wife and father-in-law for a final cup of coffee. He noticed that the old man had his spoon back in his cup.

Peterson asked, "What did the Chief want?"

"Just a social call, Dad."

"That's good. Always a good idea to stay on the right side of the police. Why, I remember back in 'thirteen, no, it must have been 'fourteen, we was going after spruce, and the Wobblies were kicking up a rumpus back at Camp Two. And I—"

Gentry abruptly got to his feet. "Sorry, Dad, I have to run. I'm late now."

The old man nodded. He was back in the woods. He shifted slightly toward his daughter and went on with the story.

Seven years could be a hell of a long time, Gentry thought. And you couldn't count on its being only seven. But, of course, it was worth it.

9545